THE MACMILLA
RELIGIOUS EDUCATION COU

GW01464512

FOUNDATIONS OF FAITH

DAVID SELF

M
MACMILLAN
EDUCATION

CONTENTS

INTRODUCTION

This is the first book of a three-year course in Religious Education. In this part of the course, we shall be exploring what it means for a person to say 'I believe...', and the events, ideas and 'messages' on which the major world faiths have been built: the 'foundations of faith'. In this first volume there is some emphasis on the Christian faith partly because it is likely to be the most immediate in the majority of localities in which the course is used. It has not, however, been assumed that the student of this course professes any particular faith or indeed any faith at all.

The course has been arranged in 27 units of study. These units are presented in groups of five and may be studied in order over the course of three terms (as shown opposite). It is not necessary, however, to study them in this order. In order to suit local syllabuses, the different groups of units can be used in other sequences, and units from the other two books of the course may be introduced into this particular year's study. It is hoped that some groups or individuals will wish to explore at least some of the topics in greater depth than is possible in what is intended to be a concise course for use in schools where only limited time is assigned to Religious Education.

It is assumed that each student has access to a Bible. Bible references are given in this form: Exodus 11:1–7. This indicates the Book of Exodus, chapter eleven, verses 1 to 7.

Rather than use the exclusively Christian terms BC and AD, the terms BCE and CE have been preferred. These stand for 'before the Common Era' and 'Common Era'. The Common Era begins with the year AD 1.

To involve more than one person in a classroom reading of the text, a number of semi-dramatised passages have been included. It may be possible to cast and rehearse these in advance of the lesson. A number of other exercises have been suggested. Several of these might usefully be repeated on topics other than those where they are first suggested. Discussion points might be explored first in small groups (perhaps with notes being made of queries and conclusions), with the small groups later reporting back to the whole class.

However it is used, it is hoped that The Macmillan Religious Education Course will lead to an understanding and appreciation of some of the ideas and teachings that have guided, inspired and encouraged different peoples and individuals through the ages.

David Self

1·I BELIEVE...?

'If the numbers on your ticket add up to 21, then it's a lucky ticket.'

'If a girl has a ticket where the numbers add up to 21, and she gives it to her boy friend, it means she loves him.'

'Or he has to give her a kiss.'

'If the last number of your ticket is seven, you'll be lucky all day.'

'The first two numbers on your ticket are the day you'll get married, the third number is the number of children you'll have...'

What do you say the numbers on your bus tickets mean?

'You'll have bad luck if you see an ambulance but don't see a black dog within five minutes afterwards.'

'If you kill a beetle, it'll be a rainy day.'

'It's unlucky to walk under a ladder.'

'Or under a railway bridge while a train is going over it.'

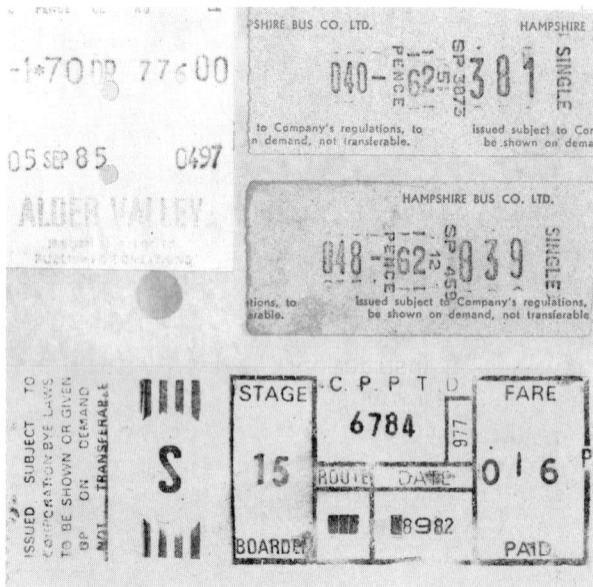

'If you break a mirror, you'll have seven years' bad luck.'

'Always cross your fingers while a funeral goes past.'

'Never step on the lines on the pavement...'

'A black cat brings you good luck.'

What do *you* say brings you good luck?

And what do you do, if you specially want to be lucky one day?

Do you know of any sportsmen or women who have particular superstitions?

What do they say in your family brings good luck – or bad luck?

A: I say Friday the 13th is an unlucky day.

B: Can you prove that?

A: Last time there was a Friday the 13th, my purse was stolen.

B: Coincidence!

A: Well, it's unlucky to walk under ladders...

B: Obviously. Something might drop on you.

Which superstitions do you believe?

Which are silly? And which silly ones do you take care not to break? Why?

Why are you doing that?

In pairs (or small groups), discuss each of the following actions. Why might you do each of these things? What do you *believe* while you are doing them? (After discussing each of them, each pair or group could report their answers to the rest of the class.)

1 Go out at your usual time on a weekday morning and wait at your usual bus stop for the bus that takes you to school.

2 Go to your doctor when you're feeling ill and then go to the chemist for the medicine you have been told to take.

3 Follow the instructions on the packet or can when making a soup.

4 Not give your friend away, even though he or she has done something wrong.

5 Jump into a river, even though you are not a very good swimmer, to rescue a much younger person.

Aries *21 March-20 April*

There are so many rumours and lies doing the rounds at work, the problem is who or what to believe. Traps will be laid by folk who'll twist things to suit themselves — you'll have to call their bluff. Your health is dodgy, so make sure you look after yourself. Avoid anything that is likely to fog your brain.

Taurus *21 April-21 May*

As much as you love someone, it's difficult to draw close to them. You've found it easy to block deep and complex sexual problems out of your mind, but the time has come when hiding no longer works. It's best to realise you must be honest about something, or run the risk of losing it completely.

Gemini *22 May-21 June*

You and your spouse or partner are at odds over family issues, and neither will give way. What doesn't help is an announcement that will undoubtedly shock you. On the work front things are much more stable, and the chances are you'll land a position that will mean more responsibility for you.

Cancer *22 June-23 July*

Something will happen to shatter your illusions, but rather than admit something is wrong you immediately put the shutters up and pretend all is well. But the longer you live in a fool's paradise and refuse to admit the truth, the more it will undermine you both mentally and physically.

Leo *24 July-23 Aug*

Don't go anywhere near financial fun and games as they'll probably backfire on you. You'll be fed a diet of get-rich-quick schemes that will leave you with

Do you believe …

Do you believe in Father Christmas?
   Why – or why not?
Do you believe in horoscopes?
   Why – or why not?
If you don't, what would convince you?

Write …

Write a horoscope for some of your friends. (Try to write one that they will believe: don't put 'impossible' things in it.)
   Exchange horoscopes and discuss them.
   If anyone believes theirs (or if one comes true), discuss why that is so.

Conclusion

What is a superstition?

2·I BELIEVE BECAUSE...

One day last spring

A: I'm going to sow these seeds in the garden.

B: Why?

A: Because they're lettuce seeds and I want to have some lettuces later on in the year.

B: But how do you know they'll turn into lettuces?

A: Because last year I sowed seeds exactly the same as these and they grew into lettuces.

B: But you can't prove that's what'll happen this time!

A: Well, you watch me sow them, and then when it's summer, come and eat the lettuces. Then will you believe me?

Every day we act on beliefs like this. We believe that if we sow some lettuce seeds, according to the instructions on the packet, then there is a good chance they will grow into lettuces. We know it has happened before. So we *believe* it will happen again – because of our experience. Just as when we follow the instructions on a packet of soup.

Other times, we trust. We do what our doctor tells us because we trust her. We *believe* what she says.

So we believe some things because of what's happened before (experience); and we believe other things because of who's telling us (trust).

But there's another kind of belief.

Father Eric Doyle

I BELIEVE IN GOD...?

When somebody says he or she believes in God, what does that mean? What sort of belief is that?

Is he or she saying:

I wonder (or I hope)	Superstition?
I know	Experience?
I trust	Faith?

This is what two Christians mean when they say 'I believe...'

> **"** When I first became a Christian, I was saying 'I hope ...' and 'I wonder' and 'Maybe'... But as I've grown to know God over the years, I've become certain. It's like two people who get to know each other. They become certain of their friendship and they know that, no matter how long they go without seeing each other, they're still friends.
>
> Now, when I say 'I believe', I no longer think 'Maybe'. I *know*. I've come to know how God helps me, to know God answers prayers and helps me when I've needed help. **"**

Michael Hastings

> **"** I think I'm saying a combination of them all. I wonder. I know. I trust.
>
> From experience, I *know* there is a God. That's what I *know*, but I don't know it like I know $2 + 2 = 4$ or how I know 'Burning is an oxidisation process' – but I know it just as I know there's something more to each of us than the atoms and cells and human body that we can see. Yes, I *believe*. **"**

Father Eric Doyle

Beliefs

Of course, plenty of other people will refuse to believe what they cannot see or cannot prove. But what Christians 'know' or believe is summed up in their *creed*. (Creed = statement of belief. The Latin for 'I believe' is 'Credo'.)

I believe in God, the Father almighty, creator of heaven and earth.

I believe in Jesus Christ, his only Son, our Lord.
He was conceived by the power of the Holy Spirit
and born of the Virgin Mary.
He suffered under Pontius Pilate, was crucified, died, and was buried.
He descended to the dead.
On the third day he rose again.
He ascended into heaven, and is seated at the right hand of the Father.
He will come again to judge the living and the dead.

I believe in the Holy Spirit, the holy catholic Church, the communion of saints, the forgiveness of sins, the resurrection of the body, and the life everlasting. Amen.

(*Catholic* here means 'universal' or 'world-wide'.)

Bob Geldof

Muslims (followers of Islam) express their belief like this:

I bear witness that there is no god but God and that Muhammad is the Prophet of God.

Sikhs believe this:

There is one God,
His name is truth.
He is the creator.
He is without fear or hate.
He is beyond time immortal,
His spirit pervades the universe . . .
He shall remain
Even if the worlds be ruined;
The King of Kings
the supreme Lord He is.

And one twelve-year-old boy wrote this when he was asked what he believed:

I believe God made Man. I believe God is invisible but a father, is a spirit that can be inside me and was once a live person called Jesus. But how can there be such a thing? That is what I keep asking myself.

Conclusion

How does belief differ from superstition?
What do you believe? Can you write out your own, private creed?

Perhaps you could collect newspaper or magazine cuttings of people who have done something brave or something which cost them time, trouble or pain – simply because they *believed* it was worth doing. You might write a caption for each one, explaining why you think the action was worth doing.

3·MAKE UP YOUR MIND

At the end of the last unit, you may have been able to write a very clear statement of what you believe. You may not have been able to do so. So how can we sort out what we think?

This is an exercise to work on in pairs. Choose one of the following two scenes. First, read it by yourself, silently. Decide whether you think Kate and Kevin are telling the truth. Don't tell your partner what you think. Next, read through the scene together, aloud, two or three times. Do Jane and Gary believe their partners or not? Are they right?

Some pairs might read or act their scenes to the rest of the class. Which Kevins and which Kates are believed?

SCENE 1

Jane: Here, what have you got there, then?

Kate: What?

Jane: That coat.

Kate: This coat?

Jane: Yeah. What is it? Rabbit?

Kate: It's synthetic. Don't hold with killing animals.

Jane: Looks all right.

Kate: Ta for nothing. Anyway, it ought to.

Jane: Why's that?

Kate: Well it cost, din'it? Hundred and fifty quid, near enough.

Jane: You nicked it then?

Kate: I never did.

Jane: Well if it cost that, how'd you get the money?

Kate: It was a present. From my Uncle Arthur.

Jane: You've not got no Uncle Arthur. I never met him.

Kate: I have. He lives Romford way.

Jane: Oh yes?

Kate: Ask me mam. He's her brother. An' I can show you the wrapping paper.

Jane: You can show me *some* wrapping paper. Anyway, what's he want to go giving you a coat like that?

Kate: He won the pools, didn't he?

Jane: Bet you can't show me the receipt!

Kate: Well, I wouldn't have it if it were a present would I, clever?

SCENE 2

Gary: Here, I didn't see you around this weekend. Where were you?

Kevin: Oh, it were great! My uncle came over and he took me and my Dad up to Norfolk in his car 'cos he knew a place where we could go fishing.

Gary: Honest!

Kevin: Yeah, and I was the only one who caught anything, and it were a dead big fish.

Gary: Go on! I don't believe you! You've never been fishing ever.

Kevin: I have! Last summer! You and me went down by that pond.

Gary: That were only tiddlers. I don't believe you. It's just one of your stories.

Kevin: Straight up! Honest!

Gary: Prove it. Where's the fish?

Kevin: Oh, we had to put it back in the river.

Gary: (*Sneers good-naturedly*)

Kevin: It's to do with conservation or something.

Gary: What colour was it then?

Kevin: Well, it was fish-coloured . . . silvery and brown.

Gary: Still don't believe you.

Kevin: It had two fins on its back and my uncle said it was a perch and he'd never seen one that big.

Gary: Anyway, I've never heard of your uncle and his fishing. You're making it up!

Kevin: Honest! We set off about 6 o'clock Saturday morning.

The evidence is...

One place where people have to make up their minds is a law court. There, the jury must decide what they believe from the evidence presented to them. They must come to the right belief.

What do you believe in this case? The scene is a juvenile court.

Magistrate: ... John William Brown, you are charged with stealing five long-playing records from the er ... Disco-Go-Go Record Bar and Snackarama, 147 High Street, on Thursday, January 29th. Do you plead guilty or not guilty?

Brown: Not guilty, miss.

The following is part of the store detective's evidence:

Store detective: ... and as store detective, I'd 'ad my eye on the accused for some time. He was standing by one of the record racks, Groups Punk and Rock, to be precise. He had several albums in his hand, ones he'd selected as cool as anything, and then he picks up his case, walks over to the cash desk, then he makes a great business of dropping his case, all sorts of things fall out everywhere, and he scuttles off out of the shop, cool as anything, as I says, without paying a penny – and when I nabs him in the street he says it was all a mistake, he forgot!

John Brown speaks in his own defence:

Brown: ... Well, I'd been looking through the records and I was really enjoying myself, 'cause I'd got this money for my birthday, and I was choosing these three albums, ones I really wanted. Anyway, I'd made my choice and then, I was taking them to the cash desk and, well you see ... My case. The fastening's been bust, and the thing is, I was in this pantomime at school ... I was one of the Ugly Sisters.

(laughter)

Magistrate: Silence in court!

Brown: Well, the thing was, I'd been told to take my costume home, to get it fitted, and all these things fell out. You know. Padding. And I was that embarrassed. Everyone was looking. People were there. They saw. And anyway, I just grabbed everything and ran. I didn't know what they'd think. And then I remembered, I'd never paid. And I was just turning back, and this bloke, the store detective, him, he nabbed me. He'd never have caught me if I hadn't stopped, you know, to come back. I mean, that proves I was going to pay ...

In juries, weigh up the evidence. Who is telling the truth? What do you believe?

Conclusions

What conclusions do your juries draw from the following 'evidence'?

There can't be a god because there's so much evil and suffering in the world.

But there's a lot of good in the world as well and there've been many good people. And think of all the wonders of nature.

If there was a proper God, there'd be just one religion.

But the fact that so many Christians and Muslims and Jews and Hindus believe in God must mean there's something in it.

Anyway, the whole of the universe is just a chemical accident – it happened by chance.

Ah, but it's all too elaborate for that, it all fits together too well to have happened by chance. Someone must have planned it.

4·HOW AND WHY

So do you think the world started by accident? And what about other questions:

Where does the sun go at night?

What happens when we die?

People have always discussed questions like these. Nowadays, scientists can give us many of the answers. It was not always so. In the past, people told stories to explain such mysteries. These stories are called *myths*. For example, there are many myths about the sun.

The ancient Egyptians thought of the sun as a god called Ra. They said he started out every morning as a young man, travelling across the sky. By midday, he was a full grown, strong man. Towards evening, he got older and older until he died. But he was always re-born the next day.

Other myths try to explain *how* and *why* the world began.

Some North American Indians used to tell a story about the Earthmaker. He was all alone. It was dark. It was always dark. He was lonely. He began to cry. He cried salt tears which flowed together to form the oceans...

Now read the first chapter of Genesis. (This is the ancient Hebrew or Jewish story of the creation.)

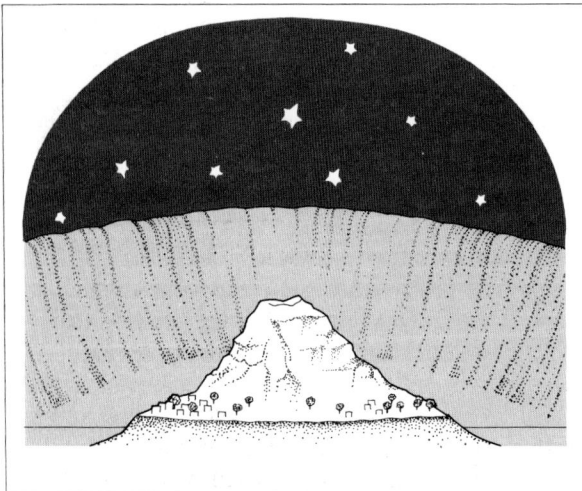

People once believed the world was surrounded by water

Creative work

You may be able to draw or paint your own picture of creation, or (in drama) you could rehearse a mimed version of one of the creation myths. (You may be able to find others in your library.)

WHAT THE SCIENTIST SAYS ...

You may know that in the past people believed the earth was flat. They also believed that it stood still and the sun and stars moved around it. An astronomer called Galileo (1564–1642) became convinced that this was not the case.

There is a play called *The Life of Galileo* by a German writer, Bertholt Brecht. In this play, Galileo explains his ideas to a young boy called Andrea. One or two of you might be able to rehearse and act this speech from the play.

66 For two thousand years men have believed that the sun and all the stars of heaven revolve about them. The pope, the cardinals, the princes, the scholars, captains, merchants, fishwives and schoolboys believed themselves to be sitting motionless in the centre of this crystal globe. But now we are travelling headlong into space, Andrea. For the old age is past, and this is a new age. During the last hundred years it has been as though men were expecting something. . . .

I like to think that it began with ships. Ever since men could remember they crept only along the coasts; then suddenly they left the coasts and sped straight out across the seas.

On our old continent a rumour started: there are new continents! And since our ships have been sailing to them the word has gone round all the laughing continents that the vast, dreaded ocean is just a little pond. **99**

An early Greek view of the world

Imagine you are Galileo. Explain to a friend (or 'pupil') what each of the pictures on these pages shows; why they were once thought to be true and why they are no longer true.

Galileo did much work that improved the early telescopes and so helped him to find out more about the stars and planets. In recent years, we have invented radio telescopes which help us to find out about space by receiving radio waves from very distant stars. There is a famous radio telescope at Jodrell Bank in Cheshire. Until 1981, the astronomer in charge was Professor Sir Bernard Lovell. The following is part of a radio interview that was broadcast when he retired:

David Self: After spending his life working as an astronomer, he's become sure of one thing. It's this. He now believes that the beginning of the universe was not an accident. I asked him to explain what evidence he has found to suggest that the beginning of the universe and the evolution of life was all part of a plan.

Sir Bernard Lovell: It is a remarkable fact that the recent discoveries have shown that even if the conditions near the beginning, which we believe to have been about 10,000,000,000 years ago, even if they were only very slightly different from what they were, then we could not exist. It is extraordinarily difficult to maintain any kind of materialistic attitude in the face of these extraordinary discoveries which are now being made.

David Self: Lastly, Professor, you've discovered an enormous amount about the galaxies, this universe, about space. Have you come to any conclusion as to why it's all there?

Sir Bernard Lovell: Absolutely not!

Conclusions

1 *How* do you think the world began? (You might ask your science teacher this question. Note: many scientists believe 'the big bang theory'. By this, they mean the universe began with an enormous explosion, and out of that explosion came all the stars and planets.)

2 *Why* do you think the world exists? (Or, *why* did that original lump of matter explode? Discuss who might help you to answer this question. And why does Professor Lovell think the explosion was not an accident?)

5·IF YOU BELIEVE ...

Professor Sir Bernard Lovell *believes* the universe did not start by accident, but he has not found out *why* it came into being. He has found no scientific proof of a creator; of God. Other people look for proof.

❝ Three days after Jesus was crucified, some of his disciples said they had seen him. They believed he was alive again. One disciple, Thomas, had not seen him and refused to believe.

'No! No, I tell you, unless I see him, unless I see the print of the nails and put my hand on the wound in his side, I will not believe.' **❞**

Christians studying the Bible

Of course if Thomas did that, he would have his proof.

When the first Russian astronaut, Yuri Gagarin, went into space in 1961, he reported back to earth that he could not see God anywhere up there. If he had, he too would have had *proof.*

But what did he expect to see? Can *you* imagine God? Is it possible to describe God? Discuss how you might try. In a painting? But how? In a poem? In music? In science? As a formula? In drama? Try to do the impossible: to describe God.

WHAT DOES IT MEAN TO SAY, 'I BELIEVE'?

To say 'I believe . . .' is to be prepared to trust. Without proof. Perhaps to trust experience, perhaps just to trust a feeling (inside yourself) that you *know* there is a God – even if you can't describe or imagine 'God'.

Many people do believe in God. But what does it mean when they say, 'I believe . . .'? That is what we shall be exploring throughout this course – and we shall see it means different things for different people.

But first: what about the two believers we have already met? What does it mean for them?

❝ I wanted to understand life. Why am I here? Why is everything else here? But when I found faith in God, that answered these problems. By believing in God, I found out why I was alive. I found out why the planet I lived on was here and I found out why it operates in the way it does. **❞**

Michael Hastings

❝ Faith, saying 'I believe in God', makes life mean something. It says three things.
(1) Life is a gift.
(2) We have been created to share our life with God and with other people.
(3) We are going to Glory, we shall be with God.
For me, saying 'I believe' makes sense of life. **❞**

Father Eric Doyle

To talk about...

What do you think are the advantages of believing in God?

And the disadvantages?!

SO YOU BELIEVE: WHAT DO YOU DO ABOUT IT?

Of course, some people do nothing about their faith.

For some, belief in God means that they must do certain things.

Holy places

People who believe in God (whether they are Hindus, Jews, Christians, Muslims or Sikhs) believe that certain places are holy.

Many believers go on special journeys (or pilgrimages) to special holy places.

They also build special holy places (e.g. temples, churches, synagogues). These are built to honour God and to be places where believers can meet to honour God. (See Book 2.)

Holy writings

Most believers say that particular books are also 'holy'; they believe that in some special way, these books contain words and ideas that have been told to us by God.

Believers read and study their holy books and treat them with respect.

For example:
Christians read the Bible
Muslims read the Qur'an
Sikhs read the Guru Granth Sahib

Believers also say that their holy books contain 'rules' or commandments about how they should live their lives.

For example:
Jews try to follow the Ten Commandments, amongst other laws (Exodus 20:1–17)
Christians also try to follow the Two Great Commandments (Matthew 22: 37–40). (See Book 2, unit 12 and Book 3, units 14 and 15.)

Belief in action

Because of the second of these commandments, Christians believe they should spend time (and money) helping others. Because of similar commandments in other religions, other believers do the same.

Your class might make a list of people (such as Mother Teresa) who, because of their faith, have spent much of their time working to help other people. Note that of course you do not need to believe in God or be a member of a religion to help others. (See Book 3, unit 19.)

With the help of local religious groups, you might find out about believers in your district who work to help others.

Twenty questions

Each member of your class or group might find out about one particular believer who has put his or her faith into action. Then, when you know enough about 'your' person, give the rest of the group twenty questions to see if they can guess who it is (e.g. Is he or she alive? Did the person work in Africa? etc.).

Mother Teresa

13

6·DARKNESS AND LIGHT

As Winter approaches, the days get shorter and colder. The sun becomes weaker: it seems that light is disappearing from the world. Darkness begins to rule...

HALLOWE'EN

66 The word *hallow* means *saint* or *holy person*, and Hallowe'en is short for All Hallows' Eve, the evening before All Hallows' or All Saints' Day, 1 November.

How is it that we celebrate Hallowe'en by thinking of witches, goblins, ghosts and spooks, and don't associate it at all with saints and holy people?

To find the answer we have to go back over 2000 years. At this point in the year, the ancient Celts held their great autumn festival which marked the end of autumn and the beginning of winter.

For the Celts, this was the end of the old year and the start of the new; and their festival, called Samhain (meaning summer's end), celebrated the time when winter and their new year started together.

The ceremonies at Samhain were conducted by the priests of the Celtic people, men called Druids. This was the time of the year when everything in nature withered and died, and so the Druids performed magic rites and offered sacrifices to their gods to make sure that life and new growth would return in the spring....

At Samhain the barriers between this world and the underworld were opened. The spirits of the human dead revisited their homes, and gods and strangers from the underworld walked abroad....

Samhain lasted for two days. It began at dusk on the evening which we know as Hallowe'en, 31 October, and ended on 2 November.

The festival began with the lighting of huge bonfires. These fires were lit to drive away evil spirits, to honour the sun, and to give thanks to

Present-day witches celebrate darkness

the gods that crops and fruits had been gathered in and safely stored for the winter months ahead....

The Christian leaders, however, were not able to think of a good way to make the autumn festival a part of the Church's calendar, and people went on observing the festival even though the magic rites and ceremonies practised by the Druids were long forgotten.

At last, in 837 CE the Church leaders decided to dedicate 1 November to the memory of all the saints in heaven and to all those whom the Church had hallowed (or made holy). The day was called All Hallows' Day.

But the belief was still strongly rooted in people's minds that the souls of the human dead revisited their early homes at this time. So the Church called 2 November All Souls' Day. It was hoped that people would say masses for their loved ones who had died and say prayers for them. **99**

Roderick Hunt

14

So we have three dates:

October 31   Hallowe'en (pagan)
November 1   All Hallows' Day (Christian),
or, as it is more often called:
              All Saints' Day
November 2   All Souls' Day (Christian)

But even after the Christian church tried to take over the autumn festival, people continued the old customs (and many are still remembered at Hallowe'en – even if only as a joke). The tradition of having bonfires at this time of year also continued until Guy Fawkes' attempt to blow up parliament. The year after that, the Puritans passed a law making 5 November a public holiday (as a thanksgiving that the plot had been discovered) and that day became the occasion for bonfires.

FESTIVALS OF LIGHT

" From the earliest time people have tried to alleviate the gloom of winter by holding mid-winter festivals. The winter solstice, when the daylight is shortest, is the time when ceremonies have often been held. The Roman Saturnalia, a winter festival of fire and light, took place from 17th to 23rd December. This was followed on 25th December by the 'Dies Natalis Invicti Solis' or 'The Birthday of the Unconquered Sun', in which Mithras, the god of light, featured prominently. It was a reminder that light would from then on begin to predominate over darkness, until spring and summer arrived.

The Romans used to deck their homes with evergreen, as a sign that life could not be extinguished by winter; they also gave gifts, often of money and gold. After Christianity had spread throughout the Roman Empire, Christians incorporated these customs into their celebrations. Jesus Christ became the 'Light of the World' whose birthday was celebrated at the same time as the pre-Christian celebrations had taken place. **"**

Geoffrey Marshall-Taylor

It is not just the Christian religion that has a 'festival of light' at this time of year. Throughout the northern hemisphere, 'winter' festivals are held to give thanks that light will, in the end, triumph over darkness; that goodness will triumph over evil. As we shall see in the next two units, Hindus celebrate Divali and Jews celebrate Hanukah.

Things to do

1 Make your own 'winter' calendar showing which days are special to you and to other people. You will perhaps be able to find useful information in a diary that you can include. Can you design the calendar in such a way that it shows how daylight lessens until the shortest day of the year?

2 Write a poem about the coming of darkness or one called 'The Birthday of the Unconquered Sun'.

3 As you study the next four units, list the similarities and differences between Divali, Hanukah and Christmas.

7·DIVALI

Divali (sometimes called Diwali or Deepavali) means 'cluster of lights'. It is a Hindu festival which lasts for five days, spread over the end of the Indian month Asvina (the last month of the year), and the beginning of Karttika (the first month of the new year). Depending on the date of the new moon, it coincides with either late October or early November.

Hindus believe there is one great spirit or power called *Brahman*. The aim of life for the Hindu is to become so good, so pure, that one becomes part of Brahman. The Hindu is helped to do this by the gods and goddesses. Two in particular are connected with Divali.

LAKSHMI

Lakshmi is the goddess of wealth. One tradition (which is celebrated especially in west India) is that, at the end of the year, Lakshmi visits those homes which are decorated with lights. She brings good luck for the new year.

Consequently, Hindu families light candles and oil lamps to attract her. This is also the time when business accounts for the old year are made up and settled: businessmen hope Lakshmi will visit them.

VISHNU

The god Vishnu is the keeper or preserver of life. Hindus believe that he has lived on earth in ten different forms. One was as Rama, a warrior and king. His story is told in a famous long poem called the *Ramayana*.

NB   Rama was married to Sita and they lived in the city of Ayodhya. Ravana was a ten-headed monster and Hanuman was the chief of all monkeys and also a god.

The story of Rama and Sita

" Because of wicked plots and rumours Rama was forced to go into exile. He tried to leave Sita behind but she forced him to take her with him, saying, 'I want to be with you: with you is heaven; without you is hell'. Accompanied by Rama's half-brother Lakshmana they went into the dangerous forest. There they met the sister of Ravana, the demon king of the island of Lanka (once called Ceylon and now Sri Lanka). She fell in love with Rama, tried to get him to desert Sita but Lakshmana, in a rage, cut off her nose, ears and breasts. She fled back to her powerful brother, crying for revenge.

Ravana set out and kidnapped Sita. For a long time Rama could not find her. It was only through the help of Hanuman, the monkey warrior, that he finally discovered she was still alive in Ravana's castle. But how could he get across the sea to Lanka?

All the forest animals came to Rama's aid. Working under the direction of a craftsman called Nala they built a great bridge. In just five days the work was completed and Rama, Lakshmana, Hanuman and their army crossed to the island. There a mighty battle took place.

After many heroic events Rama killed Ravana with the help of a magic bow made of sunlight and fire, and with a weight equal to that of a mountain. The ten-headed demon with his twenty arms lay dead.

The victorious Rama prepared to return home but he did not know if Sita had been faithful to him. Hearing this Sita wanted to die. A funeral fire was lit and she walked into the flames but instead of dying she was seen to float up out of the fire. Rama saw that she had always been true to him, rescued her and together they made the journey back to Ayodhya. The exile had lasted for fourteen years.

The story ends with the great coronation scenes of triumph. There is tremendous joy at the victory of good over evil. **"**

Howard Marsh

16

And many lamps were lit in Ayodhya to welcome Rama home.

The story of Rama and Sita is acted out (especially in northern India) during the month leading up to Divali and, at Divali, Rama's homecoming is celebrated. Huge models (some nine metres tall) are made of the Ravana. As the story reaches its end, an actor shoots a burning arrow into the model, setting it on fire in a great blaze of light.

Acting out the Return of Rama

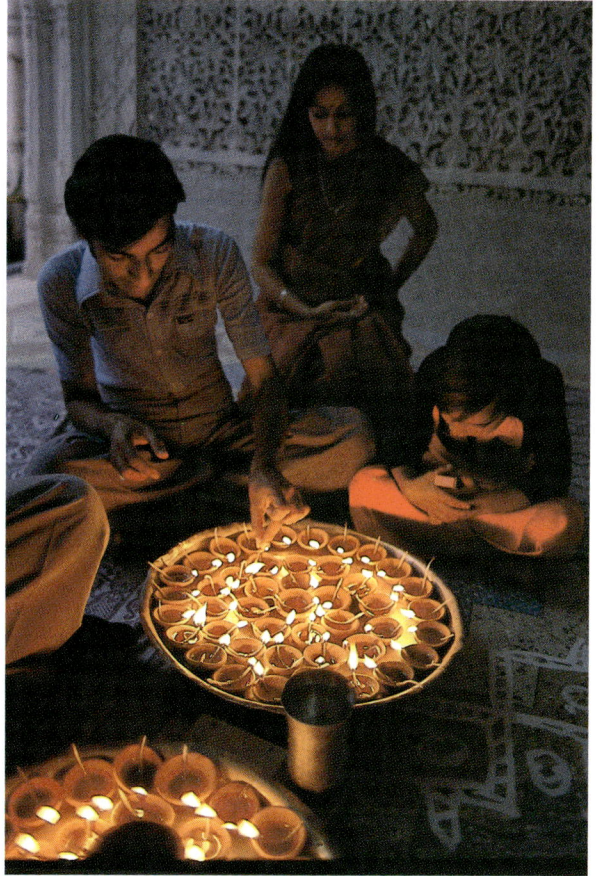

Things to do

1 Make a list of stories (including ancient and modern ones, fairy tales, legends, films, etc.) in which 'good' defeats 'evil'. Which characters represent good and which represent evil? Why are these stories popular?
2 In India, the stories of the gods are sometimes re-told in cartoon form in comics. Draw a cartoon strip to re-tell the story of Rama and Sita.

Conclusions

So Divali is a time for lighting lamps, fireworks and bonfires. It is a time for parties, giving presents and sending cards.

It is a time for making a fresh start and new resolutions, for celebrating the triumph of good over evil and the triumph of light over dark.

17

8·HANUKAH

Hanukah is the feast of lights,
Menorah's lit on all eight nights.

'Hanukah' is just one way of transcribing the Hebrew spelling. It is sometimes written Chanukah, Hanukka or Hannukah. It is also known as the 'Feast of Lights'. The menorah is a nine-branched candlestick used in Jewish homes at this time of the year.

Hanukah is an eight-day-long Jewish festival which begins on the 25th day of the month of Kislev. This usually falls in December. Menorahs are lit in Jewish homes during the festival. On the first night, the 'servant' candle (called the shammash) is lit and then the first main candle is lit from it. A second candle is lit on the second night and so on through the festival. As each is lit, prayers are said.

Special foods are eaten, parties are given and games are played. It is a time when light and happiness enliven the dark of winter, but most of all it is time for giving thanks and remembering the story of Judas the Maccabee.

JUDAS THE HAMMERER

At this time, Judah (the land of the Jews) was part of the mighty Greek empire. Even so, the Jews were allowed to live their own lives, more or less in peace, and to follow their own religion. Then a Greek general called Antiochus became the ruler of the Syrian part of the Greek empire which included Judah (the land of the Jews).

Antiochus wanted to change things and to put an end to the Jewish way of life and religion. One reason for this was that he thought that he himself was God. In the year 168 BCE, his army invaded Jerusalem. He stopped Jews from studying their holy books and observing the Sabbath. Then he ordered the sacrifice of live pigs (animals which Jews hold to be unclean) on the high altar of the Temple. Next he sent his soldiers around Judah, forcing Jews to eat pork and to offer sacrifices to himself, the 'god-king'.

Many Jews refused to do this and were put to death. However a small group of resistance fighters began to gather in the hills. Their leader's name was Judas. He was given a nickname, Maccabee (which is thought to have meant 'the Hammerer'). His followers became known as the Maccabees.

After they had made a number of successful hit-and-run raids, more men joined them. Soon they were able to fight full-scale battles against the Syrian army. Because they knew the ground better, they were often victorious and began to move nearer to Jerusalem. Antiochus then decided to put an end to them once and for all, so he gathered a vast Syrian army together. Although the Maccabees were heavily outnumbered, much to everyone's surprise, they won the battle.

Judas Maccabee led the victorious Jews into Jerusalem and they set about purifying the Temple. After cleaning it, they blessed or 'rededicated' the altar and then wanted to light the special lamp which was supposed to burn there all the time to show that God was always present in the Temple. But they could find only enough of the holy oil used in the lamp to last one day. It would take some days to prepare more. Even so they lit the lamp, in thanksgiving for the victory – and the lamp burned for eight days – by which time more oil was ready. As Jews still say, 'A great miracle happened there.'

Ever since then, every year, Jews have spent eight days celebrating the miracle of the lamp and the rededication of their Temple. Their word for dedication is 'Hanukah'.

You can read the full story of Judas and his battles in the Apocrypha: I Maccabeus 1:54–64; 3:1–9 and 42–60; and 4:1–59.

Dreidels

A popular game during Hanukah is one played with a dreidel or four-sided spinning top. These can be bought or made. A simple one can be made out of a piece of stiff card with a pencil stuck through its centre. On each face or side of the dreidel is one of the letters of the Hebrew alphabet.

The four letters which are used are chosen for a reason. They are the first letters of four Hebrew words which, translated into English, mean: 'A great miracle happened there.'

Nun	](letter)	A great	נֵס
Gimmel	](letter)	miracle	גָדוֹל
Heh	ה	happened	הָיָה
Shin	שׁ	there	שָׁם

Note: Hebrew is written from right to left so that the first letter of every word is on the right-hand side.

The game can be played in various ways. One is for each player to start with an equal share of coins, nuts or counters. A number are placed i a central 'bank'. Each player then spins the dreidel in turn.

If the letter Nun] comes up this means 'Take nothing'.
If the letter Gimmel] comes up this means 'Take all'.
If the letter Heh ה comes up this means 'Take half'.
If the letter Shin שׁ comes up this means 'Put one in'.

This simple gambling game goes on, with players adding to the central bank when it holds only one or no objects, until the winner eventually takes all the coins or tokens.

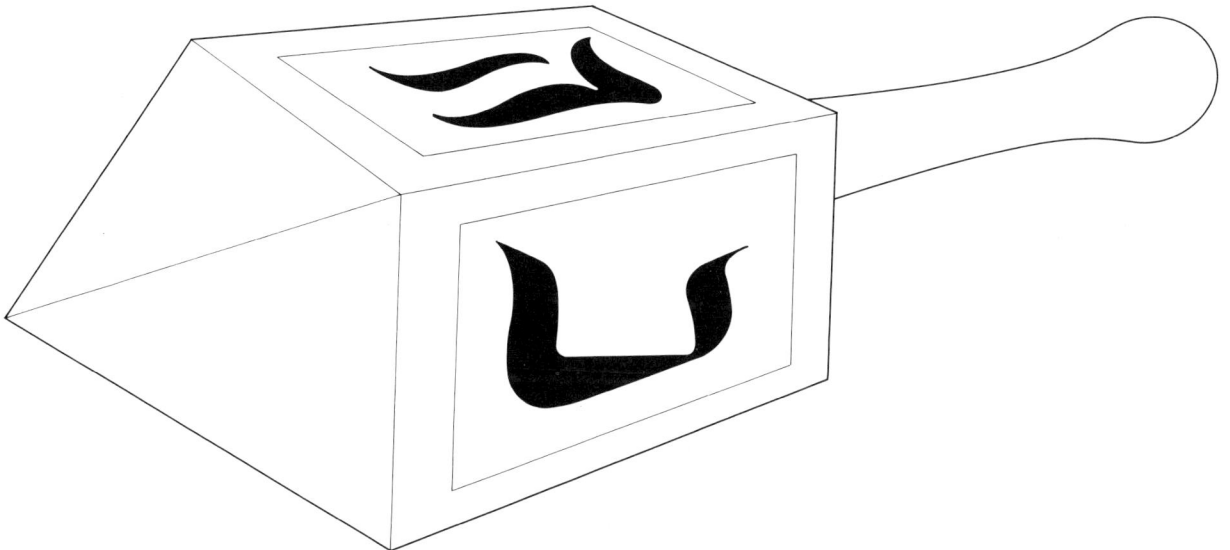

9·ADVENT

'Advent' is an old word meaning arrival or coming. For Christians, it means the four weeks before Christmas in which they think about the coming to earth of Jesus; it is a time of preparation, of getting ready.

Of course, for most people (whether they are Christians or not) this period before Christmas is a time for another kind of preparation. There are presents to be sent, cards to be written, food and drink to be bought...

As we have seen (unit 6), many traditions connected with Christmas are much older than Christianity, such as using evergreen plants for decoration and having parties.

Many 'modern' traditions come from legends connected with St Nicholas.

St Nicholas

St Nicholas was born about 300 years after Jesus at Myra in Asia Minor. He became a priest and, at an early age, a bishop. According to legend, he used a family fortune to help the poor. After his death, people sought his prayers and many miracles were attributed to him. He is the patron saint of sailors.

St Nicholas is remembered on 6 December in many European countries and especially in Holland. People celebrate the day by giving each other presents and by other customs and, in many towns, St Nicholas and his companion, Black Peter, make a procession through the streets. When Dutch people settled in the United States, they took these customs with them and Sint Niklaasje (or Sinterklaas as he is nicknamed) became known as Santa Claus by English speakers. Our idea of Father Christmas is generally said to have originated with a poem by Clement Clarke Moore, an American who saw these Dutch customs being observed in New York.

St Nicholas and Black Peter arrive in Amsterdam

> 66 'Twas the night before Christmas,
> when all through the house
> Not a creature was stirring, not even a mouse;
> The stockings were hung by the chimney with care.
> In hopes that St Nicholas soon would be there.
> The children were nestled all snug in their beds,
> While visions of sugar plums danced in their heads;
> And mamma in her 'kerchief, and I in my cap,
> Had just settled our brains for a long winter's nap,
> When out on the lawn there arose such a clatter,
> I sprang from my bed to see what was the matter 99

THE MESSIAH

For centuries Jewish prophets (or holy men) taught that God would send a 'Messiah' or 'Chosen One' to earth. He would be 'all-powerful'. He would save the Jewish people and defeat their enemies. He would relieve all their suffering and bring about a new age of peace and holiness.

The word 'Messiah' means 'anointed one'. A man who was anointed with holy oil was set apart from ordinary people to do God's work on earth. The Messiah would be chosen by God, not by men.

There are many passages in the Hebrew Bible (the Old Testament) which Christians believe describe the promised Messiah. Look up each of the following eight references and write down briefly what each says about the Messiah: Isaiah 9:6–7; Isaiah 11:1–2; Isaiah 35:5–7; Isaiah 35:10; Isaiah 40:10–11; Micah 5:2; Zechariah 9:9–10; Malachi 3:1.

Some Jews were expecting the Messiah to come at the time Jesus was born. Although some Jews did believe he was the Messiah, most did not, and of course modern Jews do not believe that Jesus was the Messiah, or that the Messiah has yet come.

So what *do* modern Jews say if they are asked what they expect of the Messiah? This is the answer of one Jewish teacher, Clive Lawton.

> 66 We expect precisely what everybody dreams of – a world of peace and of fellowship and brotherhood – where it will be considerably easier to lead a good life.
>
> The Messiah will be, we believe, a human being – not a god or even a part of God – he will inaugurate a Golden Age, an idealistic dream towards which all social reforms have tended.
>
> There are many sections of the Jewish community today who do not anticipate that this age will be heralded by an individual and they assert that the biblical prophecies referring to the Messiah are merely personifications of an age using the idiom of the period, i.e the political structure was generally orientated around a ruler – now not a necessary concept in this 'democratic' age!
>
> Whether it's an age or a person, it will be noticeably better! 99

Christians do believe, however, that Jesus was the promised Messiah. Which of the eight references that you have looked up do you think fits Jesus?

To talk about...

1 What is good and what is bad about 'commercial' Christmas?
2 Does it matter if young children believe in Father Christmas?
3 What makes a 'good' Christmas present?
4 Which of the prophecies about the Messiah do you think came true when Jesus was born?

10·CHRISTMAS

What does 'everyone' know about Christmas? What happened at the first Christmas? Without looking at the Bible, what would you say are the answers to the following questions? (You could use the questions to conduct a public opinion survey around your class, school or town.)

1 How did Mary hear she was going to give birth to the baby Jesus?
2 Why did Joseph and Mary go to Bethlehem?
3 In Bethlehem, where was Jesus born?
4 How did the shepherds hear about the birth?
5 What was the weather like?
6 Who were the men from the east?
7 How many of them were there?
8 When did Joseph and Mary return to Nazareth?

What the Bible says

The story of the birth of Jesus is told in only two of the four gospels in the New Testament. It is told in Matthew 1:18–2:23 and in Luke 2:1–40.

Working in pairs, again answer the above eight questions according to what is said in each gospel. Arrange your answers in two columns, one for each of the gospel stories. Leave gaps when there is no information.

Which of your original answers (or those of your opinion poll) are 'wrong'?

Do Matthew and Luke ever contradict each other?

What do they agree about?

Which details indicate that the birth of Jesus was, in some way, an 'out-of-the-ordinary' event?

The wise men offer their gifts: a mosaic in an Italian church illustrating the Epiphany

THE EPIPHANY

As we have seen, Matthew concentrates on the visit of some 'wise men' or astrologers to Bethlehem. They had travelled from the east (perhaps Babylonia or Persia) to the court of King Herod to find a new king. These men would not have been Jews, and so this story tells of the first non-Jews to visit Jesus. This event is now called the Epiphany. Epiphany means 'showing', so the Epiphany is the 'showing' of Jesus to the Gentiles (or non-Jews).

Why do you think Herod wanted to know what the wise men found? (See Matthew 2:1–8.)

The Three Gifts

The three gifts brought by the wise men had special meanings:

gold represented kingship

frankincense (a sweet-smelling incense) represented worship

myrrh (a precious ointment) was used during burials and represented suffering

These gifts showed that Jesus was to be a king, a priest and that he would suffer. How do Christians believe these all came true?

THE CHRISTMAS CALENDAR

We do not know exactly what time of year Jesus was born (although it is unlikely that shepherds and their sheep would spend a winter's night on the hills). As we have seen (unit 6), Christians eventually started celebrating the birth of Jesus at the time of the Roman winter festival – because people were used to celebrating at that time of the year. We know for certain that Christmas was being celebrated on December 25 by the year 336 CE. Nowadays, Christians in the west remember the various events on the following dates:

December 25 Birth of Jesus

December 28 Massacre of the Innocents (Herod's killing of the babies)

January 1 Circumcision of Jesus (sometimes called the Naming of Jesus)

January 6 Epiphany (or visit of the Wise Men)

February 2 Presentation of Jesus in the Temple

To talk about ...

For Christians, in what ways is Christmas a 'festival of light'?

A modern Nativity

Suppose Jesus had been born in modern times. How might the story have gone?

> The lights splashed off the neon lighting onto the puddles in the street. The double-decker bus jerked and two muffled figures swung off shoulder to shoulder and made their way to the park gates. Mary, one of the couple groaned, 'Ne' mind Mary,' said Josh, 'We'll find some place.'
>
> They saw ahead, through the growing darkness of the wind-swept, mid-winter afternoon, a small summer-house of a Chinese sort, and went in. Inside there was that typical disgusting smell, and the cold concrete floor was covered with litter. Josh took off his camel-coloured duffle coat and spread it over Mary, who had lain down on the carved-up green park-seat. Then he sat down beside her and tried to comfort her, but in the dark it was difficult to sound cheerful, and he fell silent.

That is the beginning of one boy's version. Perhaps you can write your own nativity story, set in modern times but showing that it is in some way a 'special' event.

Suppose there had been a Bethlehem local paper two thousand years ago. Which events would it have reported? How?

Conclusions

So Christmas is a time for lighting lamps (in shops, on Christmas trees and as decorations). It is a time for parties, giving presents and sending cards.

It is a time for celebrating the birthday of Jesus and the coming of 'Light' into the world.

So far in this course, we have learned a little about some of the different religions in the world. For example, we have considered the Hindu festival of Divali, the Jewish Hanukah and Christian Christmas. Throughout this term, we shall be studying the six main world faiths. Each can be identified by its symbol or badge:

HINDUISM OM or AUM. It symbolises what we cannot imagine, Brahman.

JUDAISM The Star of David.

BUDDHISM The wheel is the symbol of Buddhist teaching.

CHRISTIANITY The cross, signifying the death of Jesus on behalf of mankind.

ISLAM The stars and the moon are essential aids to people of hot desert countries who often travel by night. The stars guide, the moon lights the way. Islam guides and lights us on the journey of life.

SIKHISM The Khanda is the name of the two-edged sword, symbolising God's concern for truth and justice.

The following time chart shows approximately when the faiths began, and how some grew out of others:

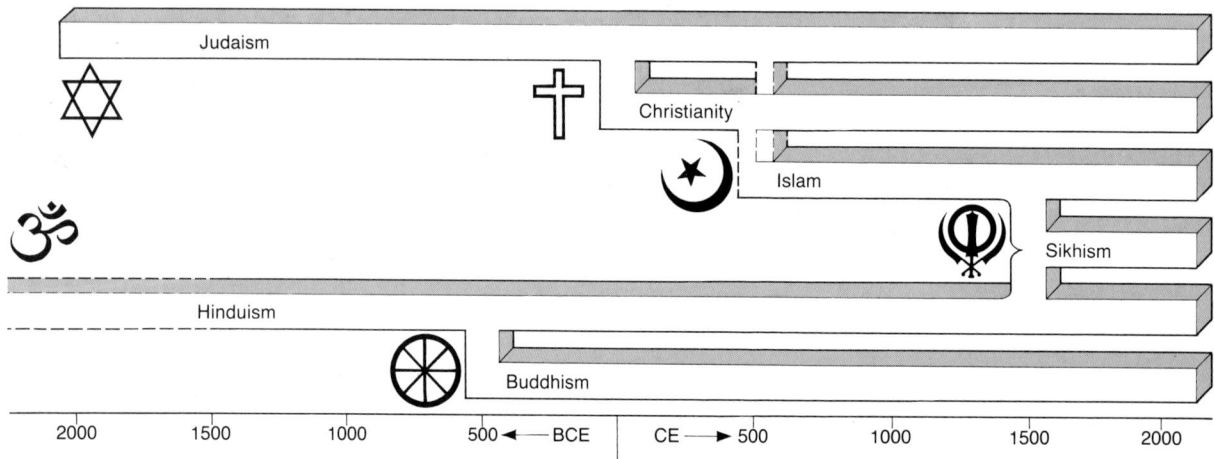

	2000	1500	1000	500 ◄— BCE	CE —► 500	1000	1500	2000

Judaism

Christianity

Islam

Sikhism

Hinduism

Buddhism

HINDUISM

With over 500 million followers, Hinduism is the world's third largest religion. There are Hindus in many countries but it is associated especially with India, the country where it began centuries ago.

Hinduism has no one founder but has been described as being like a river fed by many streams, each with its own source. Out of this variety of beginnings slowly grew the faith now known as Hinduism. This name comes from the river Sindhu, which formed the border between India and Iran (Persia) and was called the Hindu by the ancient Persians (and the Indus by the Greeks). They also called the people who lived beyond the river by the same name.

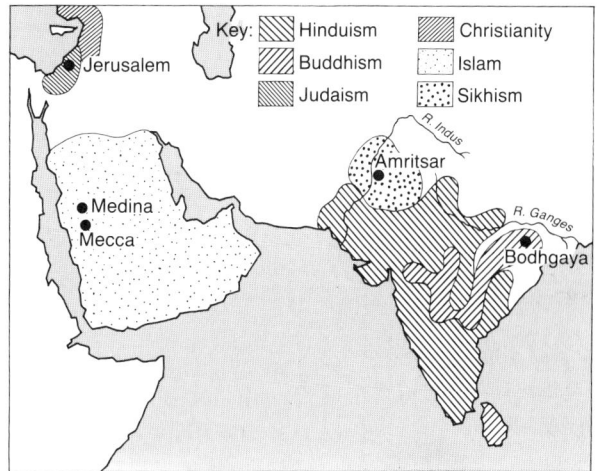

This is where the religions began and grew

Beliefs

As we have seen (page 16), Hindus believe that God is neither male nor female but a great spirit or power called Brahman. Another name for this force is Om or Aum, written:

Practise copying the symbol, and the others shown opposite. You might use them to decorate a page or cover of your notebook or file.

Hindus believe God has no form or shape but may come to earth and take a form for a particular purpose. So God can take the form of a god like Krishna or Vishnu. Some Hindus believe Jesus was God in the form of a person.

Hindus believe God is present everywhere, as this story shows:

'Explain to me, father,' said Svetaketu, 'how it is that God is everywhere, yet we cannot see him?'

'So be it, my son. Place this salt in water and come to me tomorrow morning.'

Svetaketu did as he was commanded, and in the morning his father said to him, 'Bring me the salt you put into the water last night.'

Svetaketu looked into the water, but could not find it, for it had dissolved. His father then said, 'Taste the water from this side. How is it?'

'It is salt.'

'Taste it from the middle. How is it?'

'It is salt.'

'Taste it from that side. How is it?'

'It is salt.'

'Look for the salt again and come again to me.'

The son did so, saying: 'I cannot see the salt. I only see water.'

His father then said: 'In the same way, O my son, you cannot see the Spirit. But in truth he is here.'

12·THE BUDDHA

Buddhism began in northern India. Its founder was a Hindu prince called Siddhartha Gautama who lived from about 560 to about 480 BCE.

His father tried to protect him from the harsh realities of the world and from any knowledge of suffering, by keeping him shut up inside a very splendid palace. Predictably the prince became restless.

Prince: This palace is a paradise. The rooms are as brilliant as rain clouds in Autumn. But I wish I could make a journey outside the palace, to see what the world is really like.

So the king arranged an excursion, worthy of his son's dignity. He travelled by royal chariot; and, as he travelled, he questioned the royal charioteer.

Prince: Charioteer, the people cheer me, do they not?

Charioteer: Indeed they do, my lord.

Prince: That man there. What is the matter with him?

Charioteer: He is old, my lord. That is all.

Prince: All?

Charioteer: Old age does that to everyone.

Prince: I did not realise... That is how age destroys beauty and youth and strength?

Charioteer: That is indeed the case.

Prince: Drive back to the palace. At once. How can I delight in such a journey when my heart is afraid of old age?

But nevertheless, the next day, the prince insisted on making another journey. Once again, the prince's attention was attracted by a person at the roadside.

Prince: There, beside the road. What is the matter with that man?

Charioteer: That, my lord, is a leper.

Prince: Is that what men call disease?

Charioteer: That is what disease can do to a man.

On his third journey, the prince hoped to see no more suffering.

Prince: What is that? What do those men carry?

A statue of the Buddha

Charioteer: That, my lord, is a corpse.

Prince: Is that the end which has been fixed for us all?

The prince was so distressed, that he left the palace, gave up his wealth and lived as a wandering hermit, trying to understand why there should be suffering in the world.

One day, in his search for the meaning of life, he came to a great bodhi tree.

Prince: I shall sit beneath this tree and though my flesh and bones should waste away and my life-blood dry, I shall not stir again until I have found the truth.

What is the most important thing in life? Make your own list:

The most important thing in life is...

What was Gautama trying to find?

What do you think is 'the truth'?

ENLIGHTENMENT

As Siddhartha Gautama sat under the bodhi tree, the truth was revealed to him and he became the Buddha, the fully liberated one, the enlightened one. He returned to his family and taught of Four Noble Truths and the Eightfold Path to the end of selfishness and suffering:

'When we're full of selfish wants we no longer know what the world is really like. Put aside your desires and when you've dropped those thoughts which bind you, you'll see things as they really are, and that is happiness and freedom.

'Understand yourself and the people about you properly; think how you can be of use to the world; speak the truth; be straightforward in your actions; choose a job which isn't harmful to others; try hard to find out what life is really about; take care of everybody and everything you meet; look beneath the surface of life to the mysterious source of your own existence.'

The Buddha spent the rest of his life, spreading this message, teaching and helping people. (See Book 3, unit 11.)

Meditation

The Buddha also taught people to meditate. This is not just another word for thinking.

To meditate, you need to be sitting comfortably, in a relaxed position. Then try to stop thinking. To do this, you will probably need to concentrate on one thing (such as a pebble, a leaf or flower) and not let any other thoughts come into the mind. Breathe slowly; feel your breath entering and leaving your body, allow your mind to be at peace . . .

Conclusion

'God' plays no part in this religion or philosophy and the Buddha never claimed to be anything other than a man. What he did do was to found an order of monks to spread his teaching. When they wanted to worship him as a god, he could not allow it:

Monk: Are you a god?
Siddhartha: No.
Monk: Are you an angel?
Siddhartha: No.
Monk: A saint?
Siddhartha: No.
Monk: Then what are you?
Siddhartha: I am awake.

13·THE PROPHET

Cave on Mount Hira

About 1400 years ago there lived in the city of Mecca in the country we now call Saudi Arabia a young man called Muhammad. His parents had died when he was young and he had been brought up by relatives.

Such religion as existed then in that area was primitive. It was also a fairly lawless time with much brutal fighting between families and tribes. There was also much oppression of the poor by the rich and women and children were often treated cruelly. Muhammad was however a thoughtful young man who helped the sick and needy.

When he grew up, like many Arabs of that time, he worked as a merchant and trader, trekking across the desert with a train or caravan of camels. He gained a reputation for honesty and, perhaps because of this, he was noticed by a wealthy widow named Khadijah. She gave him a job as manager of her trading business. After a short while, when Muhammad was 25, they married. Despite the fact that Khadijah was a lot older than Muhammad, it was a successful and happy marriage and

Muhammad did not take another wife while she was alive (although it was the Arab custom of those days for men to have more than one wife).

Muhammad regularly went away on his own to meditate. One of his favourite places for this was a cave on a barren hill called Mount Hira, just outside the city of Mecca.

One day, when he was about forty, he was in the cave and heard a voice calling his name. Frightened, he ran away. When he returned, he had a vision. The angel Gabriel handed him a parchment and commanded him to read (although Muhammad did not know how to read). Worried and confused, he returned home. Khadijah reassured him and convinced him that he was being called by God to be a prophet and preacher. Only after he had seen the angel several times was he really convinced. Then, over a period of three years, he had several more visions and received messages from God about what he should say and do. (Much later, he dictated these messages to one of his followers and these writings are now known as the Qur'an, the Muslim holy book.)

At the end of the three years, he felt ready to start preaching to the people of Mecca, proclaiming that there is only one God and that they should worship Him and not false idols or statues, and that they should stop their cruel ways. Some people began to follow Muhammad but most greeted his teaching with scorn and hostility. Indeed, he and his followers were attacked and persecuted. Then, in the year 622 CE, he and his followers accepted an invitation from a nearby city, Yathrib. They moved there and soon most of its inhabitants became his followers. The city became known as Medina and the Islamic calendar starts from the date of the departure (or *hijra*) from Mecca. Muslim years are described as AH (Al Hijra) and are 28 days shorter than the solar or Western year. New Year's Day 1406 AH coincided with September 16 1985.

Work out in what Muslim year we are now. When is the next Islamic New Year?

Gradually the people of Arabia were won over to Islam and in 631 CE Muhammad returned in triumph to Mecca. By the time he died in the following year, he had united the whole Arabian peninsula as one Islamic state. Within a hundred years, the Islamic empire reached from India in the east to North Africa and Spain in the west.

ISLAM

The word 'Islam' means 'submission': followers of this faith submit themselves to the will of God. The Arabic word for God is Allah.

The faith is best summed up in the basic statement of belief:

There is no god but God
And Muhammad is his Prophet.

Members of this religion are called Muslims. It is offensive to describe them as Muhammadans or to call their religion Muhammadism. They do not worship Muhammad, nor do they say he founded the faith. Although he is devoutly respected, he is only the Prophet or messenger of God.

In terms of the numbers of people belonging to it, Islam is the world's second largest religion, after Christianity.

THE QUR'AN

The holy book of Islam is the Qur'an; the collection of revelations or messages given by God to Muhammad from that first call on Mount Hira up to the time of his death.

Muslims say that the Qur'an cannot really be translated, but this is a version of its famous opening words, a prayer repeated several times a day by devout Muslims:

> **"** IN THE NAME OF GOD
> THE COMPASSIONATE
> THE MERCIFUL
> Praise be to God, Lord of the Creation,
> The Compassionate, the Merciful,
> King of Judgement Day!
> You alone we worship, and to You alone we pray for help.
> Guide us to the straight path
> The path of those whom You have favoured,
> Not of those who have incurred Your wrath,
> Nor of those who have gone astray. **"**

Young Muslims go to Qur'an school to learn sections of the Qur'an by heart – in Arabic, which may not be their own language.

Learn the opening, so you can recite it by heart.

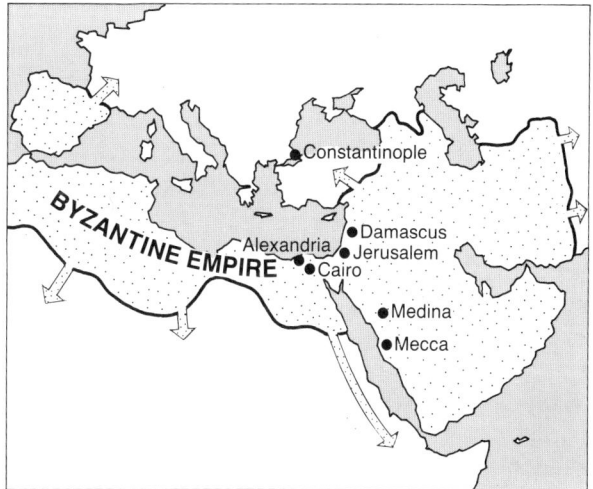

The growth of Islam

14·THE GURU

Nanak, the founder of the religion we know today as Sikhism, was born on 15 April 1469 CE, in a village called Talwandi in what is now Pakistan. The people in that area were either Hindus or Muslims. Nanak formed his beliefs from what he saw as good and bad in both these religions. For example, he disliked the Hindu caste system. He refused to undergo the Hindu sacred thread ceremony which would show he was a member of the priestly or 'high' caste. He thought Muslims were right to say that all men are equal but thought it unnecessary to face Mecca to pray.

Nanak spent his life travelling and teaching his beliefs. He became known as Guru Nanak. The word 'guru' means 'teacher'.

When he died, his place was taken by another guru. There were ten gurus and the last of these gurus, Guru Gobind Singh, founded the brotherhood of all Sikhs which is known as the Khalsa. To show that they are members of the Khalsa, all male Sikhs take the name 'Singh' which means 'Lion'. All females take the name 'Kaur' which means 'Princess'.

Besides founding the Khalsa, Guru Gobind Singh also said his successor was to be the book of Sikh holy scriptures. No longer were Sikhs to turn to a man to hear God's words but to the book. It is known as the Guru Granth Sahib and is treated with great reverence, being given a most important place in every Sikh temple or gurdwara. 'Gurdwara' means door of the guru.

There are many stories told about Nanak:

Once, Guru Nanak and a friend called Mardana were on a journey. They came to a village where everybody was rude and unkind to them. Guru Nanak and Mardana were given nothing to eat and had to sleep in the open air.

But next morning, before leaving, Guru Nanak blessed the village and prayed that all the people would stay safely in the village for ever and ever – which surprised Mardana, but he said nothing, and they went on their way.

Guru Nanak

In the evening, they came to another village where they were very well looked after: they were given splendid food and very comfortable beds to sleep in. In the morning, Guru Nanak blessed the people – and prayed that they would be scattered all over the world.

Mardana couldn't keep quiet this time.

'Why did you make that prayer?'

'Well,' said the Guru, 'wherever they go, they will do good and make other people good. And the bad people, well, it's far better for them to stay together, where they are.'

The Guru lay tired after a long journey in the open with his feet towards Kaaba, the sacred place of Muslims. A local religious dignitary, when informed, came running to him and asked him what he meant by showing such a disrespect to the house of God by turning his feet towards it. The Guru said, 'I see God in all directions. If you do not agree with me, you may turn my feet in the direction in which He is not.'

Teachings of Guru Nanak

1 There is only one God. Worship and pray to the one God and to none other.
2 Remember God, work hard and help others.
3 God is pleased with honest work and true living.
4 There is no rich, no poor, no black and no white, before God. It is your actions that make you good or bad.
5 Men and women are all equal before God.
6 Love everyone and pray for the good of all.
7 Be kind to people, animals and birds.
8 Fear not, frighten not.
9 Always speak the truth.
'O Nanak, this need we know alone
That God and Truth are two in one.'

Amritsar

The fourth Sikh guru was Guru Ram Das. He decided to build a city where Sikhs could live and work together and praise God. He chose a place, bought the land and, with many helpers, started work. Hundreds of Sikhs came to help. They built little huts in which to live and a kitchen (or 'langar') where everybody was welcome to come and eat. They dug two lakes which were called 'Pools of Nectar' (or, 'amrit'). These gave the place its name: Amritsar. In a short while it grew into a large and busy city. A temple was built and, because it is covered in gold, it is known as the Golden Temple. It has four doors, one on each side, to emphasise that it is open to all people and to show that it does not point in one direction as a mosque does. Even though all are welcome, it is a particularly holy place for Sikhs.

The Golden Temple

Things to do

1 Work out the 'moral' or meaning of each of the stories about Nanak.
2 Make up a story to illustrate one of the other teachings of Nanak.
3 Improvise or write a play about the life of Guru Nanak.
4 Collect newspaper and magazine cuttings about life in India today. Make these into a wall newspaper. (Many Sikhs live in the Punjab in northwest India. Amritsar is in the Punjab.)

15·THE TORAH

The religion of the Jewish people is Judaism. The word Judaism comes from one of the names of their original kingdom, Judah or Judaea. Throughout the long history of Judaism, there have been many leaders and prophets. Of these, the most important is Moses but the first was Abraham.

ABRAHAM

Abraham is the first of three men called 'Patriarchs' or fathers of Judaism. The others were his son Isaac and his grandson Jacob.

Jews believe that God made an agreement or covenant with Abraham about the year 1800 BCE. Find and read Genesis 17:1–8. (The name Abram means 'father' or 'respected father'; the name Abraham means 'father of many'.) As a result of this covenant, Abraham and all his family, workpeople and flocks migrated from Ur (near the Persian Gulf) where they were then living to 'the Promised Land' or Canaan. Canaan was the name then used to describe the land between the River Jordan and the Mediterranean Sea.

Abraham believed and was perhaps the first to teach that there is only one God, who created the world, and that only that one God should be worshipped.

MOSES

At some stage over the next few centuries the still nomadic Jewish people found their way into Egypt – perhaps in the search for food at a time of famine. At first they were well received. However, around 1500 BCE the Pharaohs came to power and the Jews became slaves.

Around the year 1300 BCE a new Jewish leader emerged, called Moses. There are many stories about him in the book Exodus. You perhaps know some of them. To remind yourself of them, look up and read the following:

1 The birth of Moses (Exodus 2:1–10).
2 The burning bush and the call of Moses by God (Exodus 3:1–12).
3 How Moses first asked the Pharaoh to let the Jewish people leave Egypt (Exodus 5:1–23).
There then follow the stories of the plagues of Egypt (Exodus chapters 7–11).
Exodus 12 tells the story of the Passover and the escape of the Jews from Egypt (see pages 34–5).

MOUNT SINAI

The Jews spent forty years in exile, wandering in the wilderness before they eventually reached the 'Promised Land'.

During that exile, at Mount Sinai, another 'covenant' was established between God and the Jewish people when Moses received the 'Law', including the Ten Commandments. The story is told in Exodus 19:16 to 20:21.

The Jewish word for the Law (or teaching) is 'Torah'. The word 'Torah' is also used to mean the first five books of the Hebrew Bible, which are sometimes called the Five Books of Moses. The Jewish word for their Bible (which Christians call the Old Testament) is the Tenakh.

Creative work

You may be able to tell episodes from these stories in picture-strip form, or to work as a group to make a Bayeux tapestry-style retelling of it.

To talk about ...

How would you re-word the ten commandments in modern terms, so that they apply to everyday life today (but still keep the same teaching)?

Some of course could stay as they are – but which do you think perhaps need 'up-dating'? Are there any new or extra ones you feel should be added? Why? (See Book 3, unit 14.)

Conclusions

Draw your own map or time chart showing the beginnings and growth of each of the main world religions. Include the names of important people and places. Write brief notes summarising how each religion began.

Then write one sentence for each faith beginning:

The foundation of . . . is . . .

Mount Sinai

PASSOVER

The Jewish festival of Passover (or *Pesach*) is also known as the Feast of Unleavened Bread. It begins on the fifteenth day of the Jewish month of Nisan which usually coincides with late March and early April. It lasts seven or eight days and marks God's 'passing over' the homes of the Jews in Egypt (see Exodus 11:1 to 12:39). It also commemorates the escape of the Jews from captivity and slavery in Egypt. It is a festival of independence for the Jewish faith and people.

The most important part of Passover occurs on the first (and sometimes) second evening. Then there is a celebration in the home when all the members of the family and their friends gather together for the Seder. 'Seder' means 'order' or 'order of service for Passover night'. All over the world, Jews eat the same things and say the same words (from a little book called the Haggadah) at this meal.

The table is laid in a special way. First, a fine cloth and the best dishes are placed on it. If the family can afford them, silver candlesticks are placed in the centre. There is a wine glass for each person, including the children. In the middle of the table, near the head of the family,

is the Seder plate. Near it are three matzot. These are wafers of unleavened bread (bread containing no yeast which would make it rise).

Also on the table is a dish of salt water and an extra glass that will not be used by anyone.

On the Seder plate are special foods, each with a particular meaning:

One roasted shank-bone of lamb
This represents the roasted lamb eaten on the last night in Egypt and also the lamb which used to be sacrificed in the Temple: it is not eaten.

A roasted egg
A symbol of new life. This too is not eaten.

Parsley (or other green vegetable)
This is a reminder that this is a Spring festival and it is also a reminder of the way the Jews lived in the desert. It is dipped in salt water (or vinegar).

Bitter herbs (usually horseradish)
A reminder of the bitterness of being in slavery in Egypt.

Haroset (a mixture of apples, nuts and cinnamon)
A symbol of the taste of freedom and also a symbol of the mortar used when brick-making in Egypt.

The ceremony begins with the father of the family saying a prayer and then dipping the parsley in the salt water and giving it to everyone. He then breaks a matza in two pieces. The larger part is shared and the smaller part is used later for a children's game of 'hunt-the-thimble'. As he does this, the reading of the Haggadah begins with the youngest child present asking the question:

'Why is this night different from all other nights?'

As the father breaks the matzot, he begins the story. 'We were slaves to Pharaoh in Egypt and the Lord our God brought us out from there with a strong hand and an outstretched arm . . .'

The youngest child has to ask the question:

'On this night why is there only unleavened bread?'

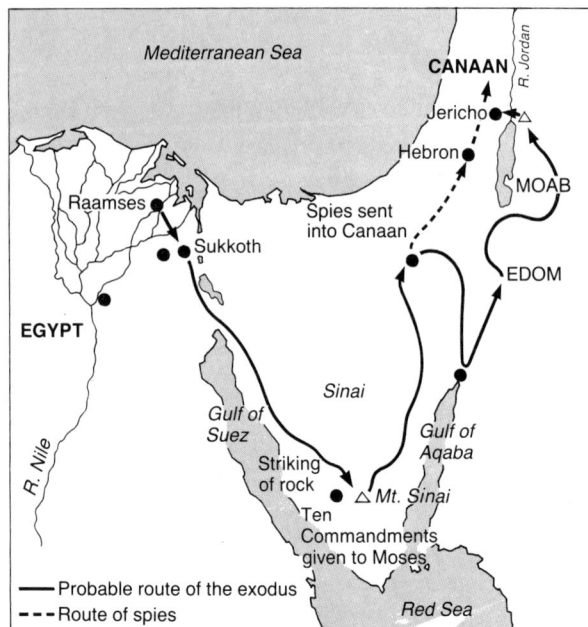

The exodus

The father recites from the Haggadah: 'We eat matzot because we had to leave Egypt in a hurry. There wasn't time to bake bread with yeast in it. We ate the unleavened bread with the roasted lamb and the bitter herbs. We were packed and dressed for the journey, ready to go at midnight.'

Wine is drunk at various times during the ceremony in thanksgiving. The spare glass is for the prophet Elijah. Jews believe that he will come back to earth before the promised Messiah comes (see page 21).

After the ceremonies, the main meal is eaten; there is much rejoicing, singing and storytelling. The Seder ends with everyone looking forward and expressing the hope that next year (or at least one year) they will eat Passover in Jerusalem:

>For all people, this, our hope:
>Next year in Jerusalem!
>Next year may all be free!

JERUSALEM

Jerusalem is a holy city for members of three religions.

For **Jews**, it is the centre of their promised land. It was here in Old Testament times that King David built his capital city. His son, King Solomon, built the first great temple here and Jerusalem became the centre of all Jewish worship. (All synagogues face towards Jerusalem.)

Solomon's temple was destroyed when the city was attacked by the Babylonians in 586 BCE, but another was built in 520 BCE, and that is the one that was standing at the time of Jesus. It was destroyed by the Romans in the year 70 CE and all that remains of it is the Western Wall.

In the Garden of Gethsemane

For **Christians**, Jerusalem is where the most important events of their religion took place. It is where Jesus taught, where he had his Last Supper with his disciples, where he was crucified and it is where his followers believe he rose from the dead three days later.

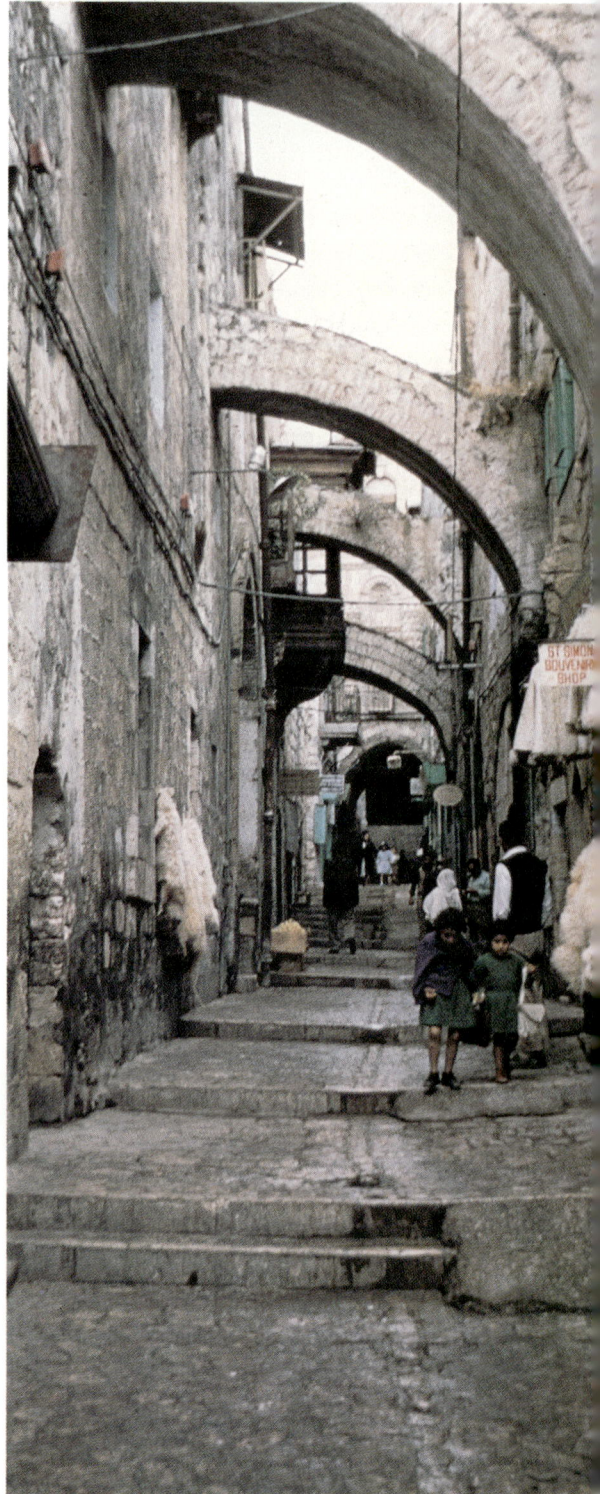

Via Dolorosa – 'the Way of the Cross'

36

The Western Wall and, beyond, the Dome of the Rock

For **Muslims**, Jerusalem is their third most holy city (after Mecca and Medina). It was visited by their Prophet, Muhammad, on his 'Night Journey'. Muslims believe that on this journey, he was led to Jerusalem where he met Abraham, Moses and Jesus; and ascended into heaven. A famous mosque, called the Dome of the Rock, stands where Solomon's temple once stood and, it is said, it is built on the stone on which Abraham nearly sacrificed his son Isaac.

Sadly, Jerusalem has not always been a peaceful place. The Jews were expelled from it; for years Christians and Muslims fought over it. In recent times, there has been more fighting there but in 1967 the whole city came under Jewish control. Now Muslims, Jews and Christians live there together. The word Jerusalem means 'City of Peace'.

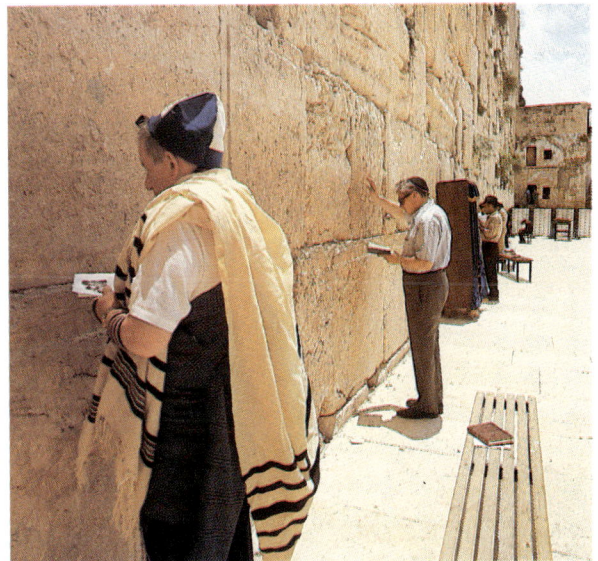

Jews pray at the Western Wall

16·PALM SUNDAY

Jesus spent about three years teaching and healing in Galilee. Then, like many Jews, he went to Jerusalem to celebrate the Passover with his closest friends or disciples. The holy day of the Jewish week is called the Sabbath (Saturday). Jesus spent the Sabbath before Passover in Bethany (see map on page 43). Then on Sunday, the first day of the new week, he rode into the city of Jerusalem, on a donkey. He was greeted by crowds who shouted 'Hosanna' (which means 'Save us, we pray') and

who waved palm branches and laid them on the roadway as a kind of carpet.

Palm Sunday is the first day of what Christians call Holy Week, the week leading up to Easter. On Palm Sunday, in many churches, Christians are given small crosses made out of palms in memory of that procession.

What did it mean?

Suppose that some years ago your country was invaded and conquered by one of the world's 'super' powers, a mighty empire. Your king or ruler was replaced with a foreigner from another part of that empire. He still rules your country, with the help of the invading army, permanently stationed in your country. The soldiers are not particularly cruel, though some rules and some of the things the soldiers and the ruler say make you very angry. You also have to pay taxes to the empire.

So what do you do? What *can* you do? Sulk? Rebel? Get on with life? What would most people do? But what might they hope would happen?

In the year 6 CE, something like that happened to Judaea. It came under direct rule from Rome. In the year 26 CE a new 'district' ruler for Judaea was appointed by Rome. He came from Spain and was called Pontius Pilate. Pilate was greedy, cruel and spiteful. Once in Judaea, he normally lived in the local headquarters of the Roman army which were in a coastal town called Caesarea. At the feast of the Passover, he came to Jerusalem to keep an eye on things. On the day Jesus entered Jerusalem, Roman soldiers would be on patrol as usual. Most Jews would respect (or fear) the soldiers. But the Jews also had hope. One day, their Messiah would come.

Look back at page 21 to remind yourself of what the Jews believed about the Messiah.

At the time of Jesus, more than ever, the Jews were hoping their Messiah would come. Would he be a military leader? Would he free them from the Romans?

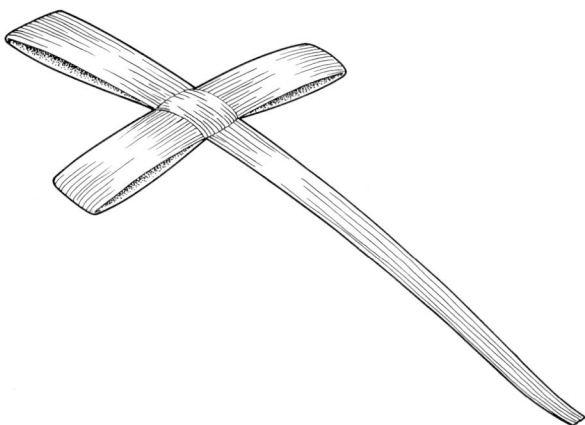

How might a new military leader enter the capital city? Riding on a strong, white horse? Ready for battle?

But the Jews knew what the prophets had said. Look at Zechariah 9:9.

And what did happen that first Palm Sunday? Read Mark 11:1–11.

So, as Jesus rode into Jerusalem, would the Romans think he looked like a dangerous new leader?

But what might many of the Jews be thinking?

Suppose you were in the crowd that day. Discuss or describe how it seemed.

In the poem, *The Donkey*, a poet imagines the thoughts of a donkey, an animal sometimes said to be particularly ugly. Despite being insulted, the donkey is happy with its proud memories of its part in the Palm Sunday story. In groups, work out the meaning of the poem.

The Donkey

When fishes flew and forests walked
    And figs grew upon thorn,
Some moment when the moon was blood
    Then surely I was born;

With monstrous head and sickening cry
    And ears like errant wings,
The devil's walking parody
    On all four-footed things.

The tattered outlaw of the earth,
    Of ancient crooked will;
Starve, scourge, deride me: I am dumb,
    I keep my secret still.

Fools! For I also had my hour;
    One far fierce hour and sweet:
There was a shout about my ears,
    And palms before my feet.

G.K. Chesterton

Try writing your own poem about another event in the week leading up to the crucifixion; or one about the wanderings of the Jews in the desert or the Passover; or one about the season of Spring and the re-birth that occurs in the world of nature.

17·IN THE TEMPLE

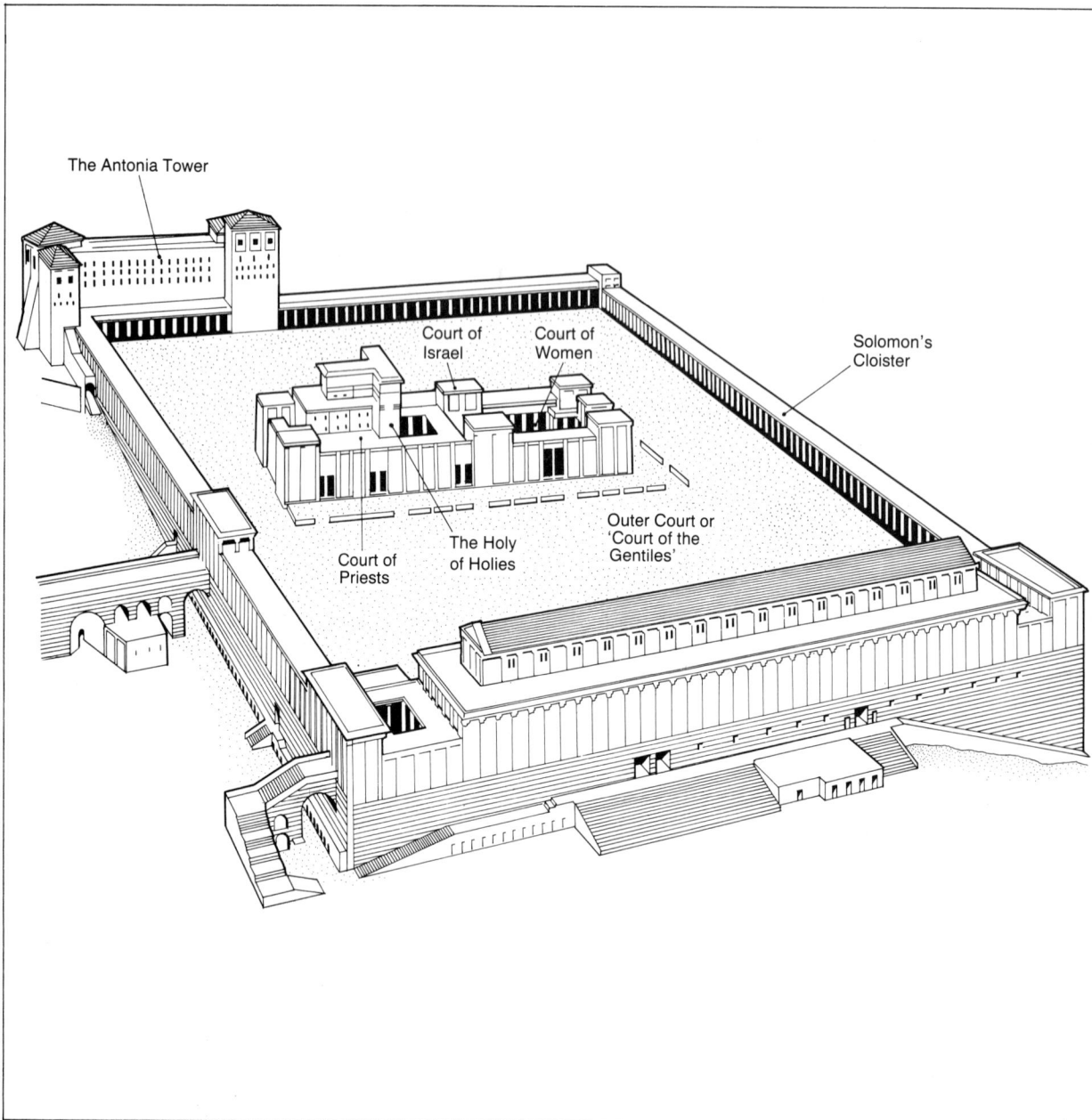

The Antonia Tower

Court of Israel

Court of Women

Solomon's Cloister

Court of Priests

The Holy of Holies

Outer Court or 'Court of the Gentiles'

During the three days following Palm Sunday, Jesus lived in Bethany, visiting Jerusalem to teach and preach in the outer courtyard of the Temple. What happened during these days is described in all four gospels, but the accounts differ in details. For example, 'the cleansing of the temple' (see below) may have happened on Palm Sunday (according to Matthew) or on Monday (Mark). Remember that the gospels were written some years after the life of Jesus and different details would then seem important to the different writers.

Suppose four of you were to write detailed accounts of the last week of last Summer term. Would each description be the same?

What is surprising is that the four gospel accounts are so similar.

THE SECOND TEMPLE

The first Jerusalem Temple was built about a thousand years before the life of Jesus, by King Solomon. In the year 586 BCE, the Temple was destroyed by King Nebuchadnezzar, King of Babylon. It was rebuilt about sixty years later but was not as splendid as it had been.

In 20 BCE, King Herod started a complete rebuilding of what became known as Herod's Temple or the Second Temple.

The Temple occupied about one-sixth of the city: 14 hectares (35 acres). See the map on page 45. It was built of white limestone and decorated with gold. It stood on an enormous level platform. Constructing this was an impressive engineering feat because the ground fell away in the east down towards the Kedron valley. Here the platform had to be supported on arches, in places as much as 45 metres above the ground.

In 70 CE, the Temple was destroyed by the Romans. The platform still remains and still dominates the old city of Jerusalem. Nothing else remains, except part of the Western Wall. (See pages 36 and 37.)

Visiting the Temple

Jewish families often made special visits to the Temple to offer a sacrifice to God. The sacrifice might be of an animal, vegetables or incense. For example, a poor woman might offer a pair of birds as a sacrifice. Anyone visiting the Temple would first enter the Court of the Gentiles. Here they would find ritually clean animals on sale, ready for sacrifice. As the ordinary coins in everyday use were Roman and showed the head of the Roman emperor, they were not used in the Temple. Moneychangers therefore set up stalls in the Court of the Gentiles where Roman coins could be changed for special Temple ones which were then used to buy the sacrificial animals.

They could also be used as offerings and were put in the 'Treasury' or treasury chest.

Any Jew visiting the Temple would then go into the Women's Court. Women and young boys waited here while adult male members of the family went on into the narrow Court of Israel. From here they could look out at the altar where their offering would be sacrificed by the priests. Certain parts of the offering were always burned.

Cleansing the Temple

According to Mark, Jesus visited the Temple on Monday of Holy Week. Read Mark 11:15–19.

Tuesday

Again according to Mark, Jesus also spent the Tuesday in the Court of the Gentiles, speaking to the crowds who gathered to listen to him. (Why is it most unlikely he did this in any other part of the Temple?)

Read carefully three sections of Mark's description of that day:
(a) The Parable of the Vineyard (Mark 12:1–9).
(b) The Roman coin (Mark 12:13–17).
(c) The widow's offering (Mark 12:41–44).
Jesus often told 'parables' like the one about the vineyard and its owner. Can you work out its meaning?

Re-tell the meaning of the story straightforwardly and not as a parable. Can you make up a modern parable that has the same meaning?

Suppose you were one of those sent to ask Jesus the 'trick' question about the Roman coin. What would you say when you had to report back about what happened?

Projects

1 Write or tell a story in which a family return home from visiting Jerusalem for the Passover. They tell their friends about what they saw and heard on the first three days of the week before Passover.
2 Suppose one of Jesus's followers kept a diary. Write the entries for the Sunday, Monday and Tuesday.

41

18·MAUNDY THURSDAY

If we rely on Mark's account of what happened, Jesus probably spent the Wednesday of that week in Bethany (Mark 14:3–9. See map on page 43.) As becomes clear from the various gospels, several women were among the close followers of Jesus.

In Britain, the Thursday of Holy Week is called Maundy Thursday. 'Maundy' comes from a Latin word, 'mandatum', which means commandment. On this day, Jesus gave his followers a new commandment: 'Do this in memory of me . . .'

Jesus presumably knew that the priests were by now plotting to arrest him and so did not return to Jerusalem till the Thursday evening, perhaps as it was going dark.

Tradition says that Jesus and his twelve closest followers (or disciples) gathered in an upper room (or guest room) in the house of Mark's mother and that it was Mark who led Peter and John to the house (Mark 14:13–16).

The gospels describe the supper they ate that evening as a Passover meal. Not everyone agrees with this as there is no mention of the lamb or other items that would have been part of the meal.

It was however at this meal that Jesus gave his followers a new command:

Jesus, in the same night in which he was betrayed, took bread and when he had given thanks he broke it and said, '*Take, eat, this is my body which is being broken for you. Do this in remembrance of me.*' Similarly, when supper was ended, he took the cup saying, '*This cup is the new agreement in my blood: do this, whenever you drink it, in remembrance of me.*'

Read Mark's account of the meal (Mark 14:17–26). (See also Book 2, unit 14.)

For most Christians, remembering or celebrating this Last Supper is a most important part of their faith. Some churches call it Communion (which means 'sharing'), some call it the Eucharist (a Greek word meaning 'thanksgiving'), Roman Catholics call it Mass and others call it the Lord's Supper or the Breaking of Bread.

The artist Leonardo da Vinci's painting of the Last Supper

WHO'S WHO

The Sadducees

A Jewish political party, committed to defending the interests of the priesthood and wealthy and aristocratic Jewish families. They were determined to hold on to what power remained to them under the Romans. The chief priest, Caiaphas, was a Sadducee (as was his father-in-law, Annas, who had been chief priest before Caiaphas).

The Pharisees

Devout, educated men, opposed to the Sadducees. Some Pharisees were critical of Jesus, just as he was opposed to their strict (and sometimes narrow) interpretation of the law. Although they were sometimes intolerant, they were also respected and often popular.

The Sanhedrin

This was a council of seventy 'elders'; the supreme Jewish court. Under Roman rule, it had limited power and probably could not impose the death penalty. The Sadducees had a $\frac{2}{3}$ majority over the Pharisees on the Sanhedrin.

The Romans

The whole of Palestine was under Roman rule. Parts were administered by Philip and Herod Antipas, sons of the partly Jewish King Herod (who had ruled at the time of the birth of Jesus). Philip and Antipas were given the title 'king' but were really tetrarchs, 'puppet' rulers appointed by Rome.

Judaea (see map) was ruled not by a local 'king' but by a Roman governor, Pontius Pilate. When in Jerusalem, Pilate stayed in what had been King Herod's palace. It is uncertain where Antipas stayed on his visits. Note that when Pilate was trying to avoid sentencing Jesus, he sent him to Herod Antipas because Jesus came from his area.

The Zealots

Zealots were extreme revolutionaries, freedom fighters who wanted the Romans out of Palestine. To them, paying tax to Rome was worse than slavery. Their motto was 'No friend but the Zealot, no tax but the Temple tax, no king but God alone.' It has been suggested that Judas (who betrayed Jesus) and Bar-Abbas (who was set free instead of Jesus) were both Zealots. Some people think that when Judas

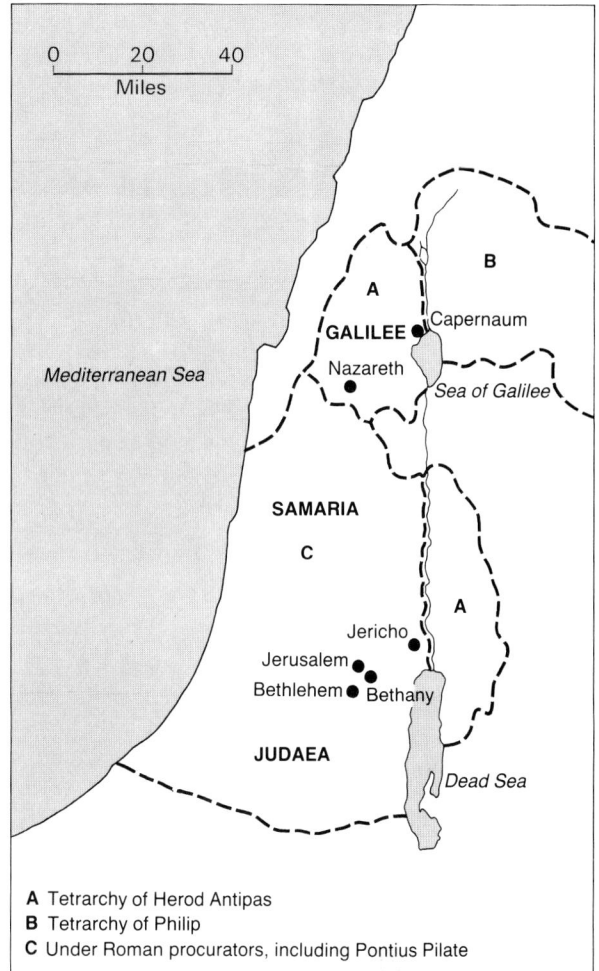

A Tetrarchy of Herod Antipas
B Tetrarchy of Philip
C Under Roman procurators, including Pontius Pilate

Palestine in the time of Jesus

betrayed Jesus he was trying to provoke Jesus into leading a revolt against the Romans. Some Zealots were also known as 'sicarii' or 'daggermen': hence Judas's other name, Iscariot.

Arrest, accusations and trials

Using the time chart and map on pages 44 and 45 and the gospel accounts (for references see the time chart), work out exactly what happened between the Last Supper and the Crucifixion.

So far as you can tell, where were each of the main characters, at each stage of the story? Re-tell the story in your own words. Or tell it from the point of view of one of those involved.

What do you think?

1 Why was Jesus not arrested earlier in the week? (Did the priests not know where he was?)

2 Why was the arrest made in secret?

3 Why do you think the priests needed the help of Judas Iscariot?

4 What other problems did the priests have?

5 Why the hurry?

6 Do you think the trial before the priests was 'fair'?

7 Of what did they finally accuse Jesus?

8 Of what did the priests first accuse Jesus when they brought him to Pilate?

9 Pilate was a tactless, obstinate, ruthless man. He had passed the death sentence many, many times before. Why was he apparently so keen to let Jesus go free?

10 John's gospel gives a much more detailed account of the trial before Pilate (John 18:28 to 19:22). What made Pilate finally condemn Jesus to death?

11 What was Pilate's 'official' reason for finding Jesus 'guilty'? Do you think the trial before Pilate was 'fair'?

12 If Judas was prepared to betray Jesus, why do you think he regretted it so soon afterwards? (Matthew 27:3–10.)

The Last Hours (times are approximate)

	Mark	*Matthew*	*Luke*
Thursday *6 p.m. The Last Supper* Final meal for Jesus and disciples in Jerusalem. Jesus talks of his coming death; says he will be betrayed by a disciple. Jesus asks disciples to remember the Last Supper.	14:12–26	26:17–30	22:7–39
8 p.m. Jesus and disciples go across Kidron Valley to Mount of Olives. In Garden of Gethsemane he suffers mental torture. Judas leads men who arrest Jesus.	14:32–52	26:36–56	22:39–53
Friday *3 a.m.* The Jewish Authorities examine Jesus. Witnesses cannot agree; authorities do not understand Jesus, and accuse him of blasphemy. Outside, Peter denies having known Jesus.	14:53–72	26:57–75	22:54–62
6 a.m. Authorities, needing Roman approval, accuse Jesus of treason. Pilate seems unconvinced. Bar-Abbas released; Jesus sent for execution.	15:1–15	27:1–26	22:66 to 23:27
8 a.m. Jesus is mocked and tortured. Crown of thorns. He is whipped.	15:16–20	27:27–31	
9 a.m. Jesus is led to Golgotha, too weak to carry his cross. Refuses any drug. Crucified with two criminals. Mocked and insulted by crowd.	15:21–32	27:32–44	23:26–45
Noon to 3 p.m. A strange darkness. Curtain of Temple split in two. Jesus dies.	15:33–41	27:45–55	23:46–9
3 p.m. till 5 p.m. Joseph of Arimathaea asks for the body. Body placed in stone tomb. Certain women note the place.	15:42–7	27:57–61	23:54–6

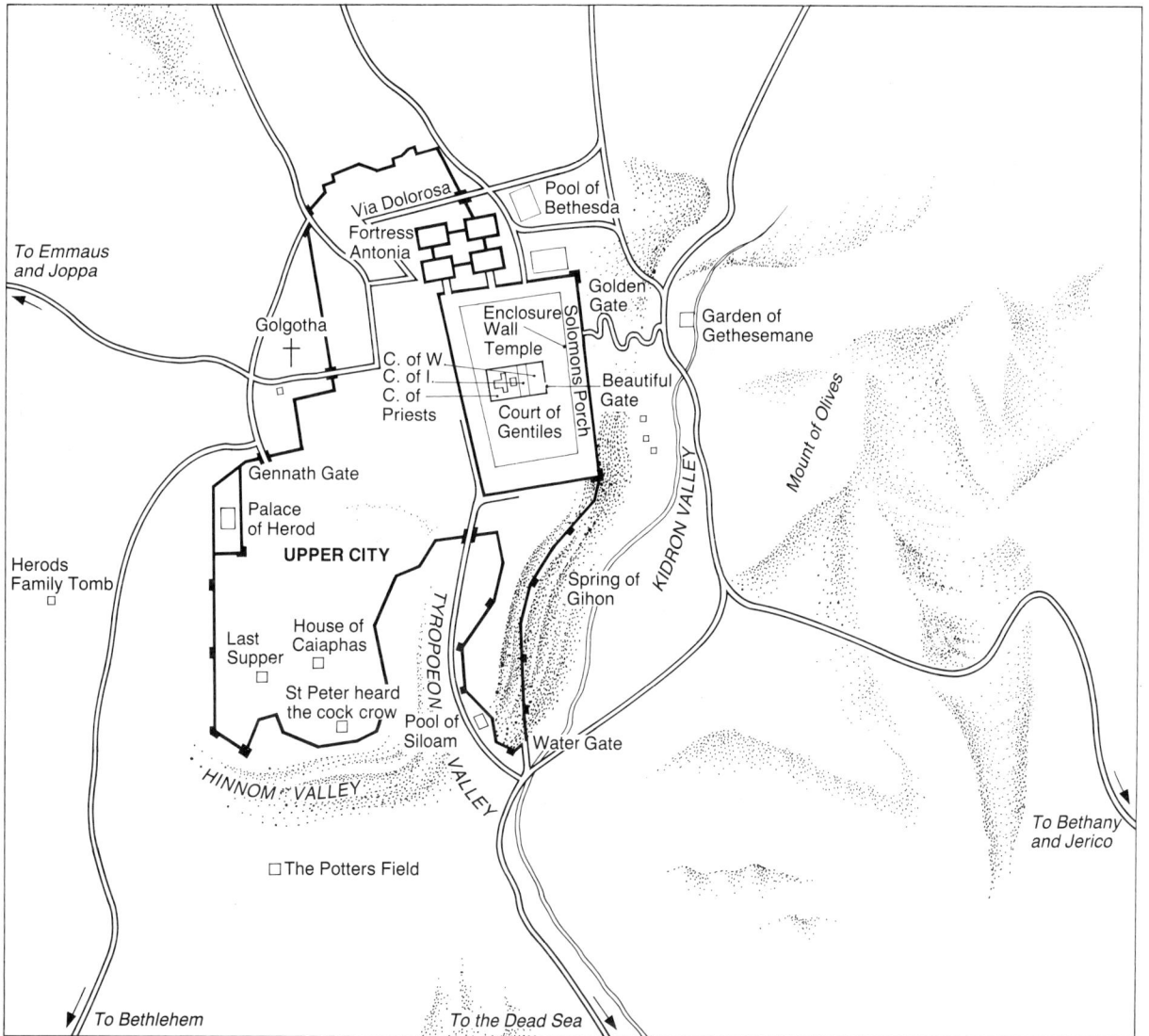

The map shows Jerusalem in the time of Jesus with the following labels:

- Via Dolorosa
- Pool of Bethesda
- Fortress Antonia
- To Emmaus and Joppa
- Golden Gate
- Garden of Gethesemane
- Golgotha
- Enclosure Wall Temple
- Solomons Porch
- C. of W.
- C. of I.
- C. of Priests
- Court of Gentiles
- Beautiful Gate
- Mount of Olives
- Gennath Gate
- KIDRON VALLEY
- Palace of Herod
- UPPER CITY
- Herods Family Tomb
- Spring of Gihon
- TYROPOEON VALLEY
- House of Caiaphas
- Last Supper
- St Peter heard the cock crow
- Pool of Siloam
- Water Gate
- HINNOM VALLEY
- To Bethany and Jerico
- The Potters Field
- To Bethlehem
- To the Dead Sea

Jerusalem in the time of Jesus was considerably smaller than it is now. It was walled and bounded in the east by the Kidron Valley. 'Kidron' comes from a Hebrew word meaning dark or shady and refers to its depth.

When Jesus had been arrested, which way do you think he was brought back into the city? Along the valley and through the Water Gate or through the Temple and the middle of the city?

The trials in front of the priests are thought to have taken place in the house of Caiaphas; those in front of Pilate would have been at Herod's palace. Outside the palace was a raised platform (or 'tribunal') from where the governor could address the people. Jesus was presumably taken to the Roman fortress (Antonia Fortress) north of the Temple before being taken along the Via Dolorosa to Golgotha (then outside the city walls) to be crucified.

19·CRUCIFIXION

Crucifixion was described by the Roman orator Cicero as the most cruel and frightful sentence. It was used by the Romans to punish murder, banditry and especially rebellion.

The victim was first scourged with a 'flagrum' (a whip with two or three thongs with pieces of bone or metal attached to the thongs). The victim next had to carry the cross-piece of the cross to the place of execution. The upright was kept ready, in position. The victim was then nailed to the cross-piece through the lower arms. The beam would then be raised and fixed to the upright. The nails would tear through the arms outwards to the wrists. The feet were then nailed to the upright. The cross sometimes had a tiny ledge on to which the victim could haul himself up and sit. This would prolong the agony. He was occasionally offered drugged wine. A placard describing the crime was fixed on the cross.

Death would eventually occur because of loss of blood, heart failure or suffocation (caused by the body's weight being taken on the arms). Victims might take up to a week to die. If it was decided to speed up the execution, the victim's legs were broken against the cross.

The priests wanted Jesus (and the others crucified with him) to be dead and removed from the crosses before the start of the Sabbath (6 p.m.) so that the festival would not be defiled. Pilate gave permission for the legs to be broken, but the soldiers found that Jesus was already dead. Despite the fact that he was on the cross for a comparatively short length of time, there seems no doubt that he did die. The Roman soldiers would have seen many such executions and would have had little doubt about the matter (see Mark 15:44–5). John's gospel (19:31–7) records that the soldiers found that Jesus was indeed dead but one of them 'checked' by piercing his side with a spear.

Project
Study the gospel accounts of the crucifixion of Jesus and make a note of what Jesus is recorded as saying while being crucified.
NB Time was measured from sunrise: the first hour was 6 a.m. and so the sixth hour was mid-day, and so on.

Who said that?
Who said (or might have said) the following? Can you work out where and when each remark might possibly have been made?

66 We didn't know what was going on. Last night, Jesus and the men . . . his disciples, they had supper. And then they were going out of the city. You know, outside the walls. We didn't know anything. Then we heard, people were saying, he'd been arrested. And now he's up on trial. At the High Priest's. 99

66 We are thinking only of the good of the Roman Empire. This man, Jesus from Nazareth, is trouble. His teaching has started riots. And might I point out, he has made no denial, no denial, of the charge that he claims to be a king. As you know, we have no king but the Emperor Tiberius. 99

66 You were right. I am from Galilee. Last night, he said we'd run away. I said I wouldn't. Never. And then, after he was arrested, I got back into the city. Into the High Priest's house. They asked if I was one of his friends. I said . . . I said I didn't know him. 99

" I should like to make this absolutely clear. I wash my hands of this affair. I am not responsible for the death of this man. Take him. Take your . . . your 'king'. **"**

News summaries

Suppose there had been a local radio station in Jerusalem at the time of Jesus.

Try writing the one-minute hourly news summaries that might have been broadcast throughout the day.

Which one might end as follows?

'And lastly, weathermen have as yet no explanation for the unnatural darkness which began about an hour ago. As listeners in Jerusalem will know, at the moment it is hardly light enough outside to read a scroll.'

20·EASTER

Christians believe that 'on the third day, he rose again': that is, on the Sunday morning after he was crucified, Jesus came back to life. A word sometimes used for this is 'resurrection'.

For Christians, Easter Sunday, when they celebrate this belief, is the most important day of the year. They go to church and most receive holy communion. In Greece especially, Christians proclaim their faith in the way they greet each other on Easter morning:

'Christ is risen!'

'He is risen indeed!'

('Christ' comes from the Greek for the Hebrew word, 'Messiah'. It means the 'anointed' one.)

Did he rise from the dead?

Read Mark's account of the burial of Jesus and his description of what happened early on the Sunday morning (Mark 15:39 to 16:8).

So did Jesus rise from the dead?

There are various possibilities:

1 The women went to the wrong tomb.
2 Jesus did not die on the cross and with (or without) other people's help, managed to escape from the tomb.
3 His followers (perhaps Joseph of Arimathaea) took the body away and hid it; and then told everyone that Jesus had risen from the dead.
4 The priests stole the body.
5 The Romans hid the body.
6 The disciples only thought they saw Jesus again.
7 He did rise from the dead.

Discuss what you think are the arguments for and against each of these theories.

The Turin Shroud

There is in the cathedral of Turin a shroud or burial cloth. Some people believe it to be the shroud in which Jesus was buried.

The ivory-coloured cloth measures 4.36 metres by 1.10 metre. On it is the full-length imprint (in negative) of a bearded crucified man who has been laid to rest lengthways on one half of the cloth. The rest of the cloth has been loosely draped over the head and laid on top of the body. The marks show that his back has been scored by the application of a leaded whip; there are traces of blood-flow from the wrists, feet, side and head – these latter consistent with the wounds that would be caused by a spiky cap or crown being rammed down onto the scalp. Unlike most victims of crucifixion, this man's legs have not been broken.

Scientists are unable to say what caused the marks. They are neither paint nor any known pigment; they do not penetrate the cloth, but are rather like scorch-marks.

Its exact age has not yet been proved. There is nothing to disprove the suggestion that it dates from the first century CE, and is certainly at least 600 years old. Its fibres are like those cultivated in the Middle East, and traces of pollen found only in Palestine have been discovered in the cloth.

If the Turin Shroud is a mediaeval forgery, no one has been able to show how it was done. Forgery or not, it is a precise and moving picture of a man crucified according to Roman custom and with details that match those of the Gospel narrative. To some it is merely a curiosity; to others it is a 'photographic negative' of the crucified Christ; and to still others the Shroud bears an imprint of the moment of the Resurrection, the marks scorched on the cloth by the heat radiated at that moment.

Part of the Turin Shroud, showing the imprint of the face of the crucified man

21·THE FIRST DISCIPLES

For about three years, up to his crucifixion, Jesus travelled around Galilee and Judaea (see map on page 43) preaching, teaching and healing. For almost all this time he had twelve close friends or followers with him. They are called the Twelve Disciples or Twelve Apostles.

The word 'disciple' means 'follower', someone who accepts and follows the teaching of another.

The word 'apostle' means 'messenger' or someone who is sent away to spread news or a message.

While Jesus lived on earth, the Twelve were learners *or disciples. Later they became* teachers *and spread his message in many different towns and countries: they were then* apostles.

The four Gospels do not tell us many facts about them and they are even called by different names or nicknames on various occasions. Their names are listed three times in the Gospels (Matthew 10:2–4; Mark 3:16–19; and Luke 6:14–16) and also in the book called Acts of the Apostles (1:13).

Compare the lists. Note that this does not necessarily mean one list is 'wrong'. Suppose four people in your class wrote down a class list from memory. How might those lists differ? Copy out the table and use a Bible to replace the references with the correct information.

The call of the disciples

From the beginning, Jesus obviously knew that he could not do what he wanted to do without help. Very early on in those three years, he chose or 'called' his disciples. The story of how he chose some of them is told in three places in the Gospels (Mark 1:16–20; Luke 5:1–11; and John 1:35–42).

What else?

What else do you know about the Twelve Disciples? What other events in the Gospel story do you know that involved particular ones?

Write brief notes on Simon Peter, Andrew, John, Judas Iscariot, Thomas and Matthew.

Name	Surname or other names	Father	Home	Business
Simon	Peter	*Jonah*	Capernaum	*Luke 5*
Andrew				*Mark 1*
James ('The Elder')	'Boanerges' or 'Sons of Thunder'	*Mark 1:20*	Bethsaida	*Luke 5*
John				
James ('The Younger')	James the Less	*Luke 6:15*	Galilee	
Jude or Judas	also known as Thaddeus or Lebbaeus			
Philip			*John 1:43*	
Nathaniel	Bartholomew		Cana	
Matthew	*Luke 5:27*		Capernaum	*Matthew 9:9*
Thomas	*John 20:24*		Galilee	
Simon	*Luke 6:15*		Galilee	
Judas	*Matthew 10:4*	*John 6:71*	Kerioth of Judaea	Revolutionary?

And then there were eleven...

Some time after the resurrection, the eleven remaining 'special' disciples (or apostles) decided that they should make up their numbers to twelve again. They felt that the 'new' apostle should be someone who was 'a witness, with us, of the resurrection'. They selected two men, Joseph Barsabus and Matthias. They then prayed that they should make the right choice between these two, and then they voted. Matthias was elected, 'and he was numbered with the eleven apostles'.

St John and St Peter by the artist Raphael Santi

22·APPEARANCES

In the forty days following Easter, the disciples believed that, on a number of occasions, Jesus appeared to them. Despite having been crucified, he now appeared to be alive again. Possible or not?

We can read reports of these appearances in the Gospels. Copy out the table and use a Bible to help you to fill in the details of five of these appearances. (In the column headed 'And the consequence was...', write down what effect the appearance had on those who saw Jesus. For example, what did they believe or do?)

So what really happened?

There seems little doubt from the various stories in the Gospels that the disciples really *believed* that Jesus had come back to life; they believed in the 'resurrection'. Some of those disciples would have said they not only *believed* but that they also had evidence or proof.

But problems remain. What about the two disciples on the road to Emmaus? This is what one writer has had to say:

" ... despite his walking with them for some distance, the two people on the road to Emmaus did not recognise Jesus until he had entered their house. He took bread, blessed it and broke it. Then they knew who he was, and were very startled. As soon as they recognised him he vanished. They immediately rushed back to Jerusalem with the news... Could Jesus really have revived and recovered from his wounds and appeared to them in his body that had died? They might well have known from his other healings that Jesus could probably have healed himself too – but how could they explain the fact that he had walked with them for miles, talking with them, and they had not recognised him – and then suddenly they did? Had he somehow been able to change his shape before their very eyes? And how had he just disappeared? **"**

Rosalyn A. Kendrick

Reported appearances

	Reference	Where?	To whom?	What did Jesus do?	And the consequence was...
1	Matthew 28:1–8 Mark 16:9–10 Luke 24:1–10 John 20:1–18	Jerusalem, outside the tomb	Mary Magdalene and the other women		
2	Mark 16:12–13 Luke 24:13–33	On the road to Emmaus			
3	Luke 24:34	Jerusalem	Simon Peter		
4	Luke 24:36–49	Jerusalem			
5	John 20:19–29				

Improvisation

In pairs, imagine you are those two disciples. Improvise the conversation you have on the way back to Jerusalem: talk over what happened and what still puzzles you.

Back in Jerusalem

When those two disciples arrived back at Jerusalem, they found Simon Peter had also seen Jesus:

> **"** How did Jesus appear to Peter before the Emmaus disciples got back to Jerusalem? Is it possible that he could have 'dematerialised' in Emmaus and then 'rematerialised' in Jerusalem? How did he suddenly appear in the upper room? We are given to understand that the doors were shut, which probably meant *locked*, for fear of the Jews. Does this not suggest that Jesus just materialised? Or perhaps, like a traditional ghost, he came through the wall. **"**

So what do you think happened?
And remember what happened next:

> **"** While they were discussing the implications of all this, Jesus suddenly appeared again. This time they all saw him, and they were terrified! To prove that he was not just a ghost, he took some broiled fish and ate it. He led them out to Bethany, promised them that they would soon be 'clothed with power from on high', told them they were to stay near the Temple, blessed them, and disappeared. **"**

The stamp test

A Christian magazine once suggested that its readers should take a postage stamp and write their main beliefs on the back of it. What do you think the apostles would have written if they had been asked to do this (after the 'appearances' of Jesus)? Obviously there is very little room and they would only have been able to put the main points.

Take a piece of paper the size of an ordinary stamp and try writing what you think the apostles would have written. (Look back at page 7. How much of the Christian creed can you write on the back of a stamp?)

If you were asked to write what is important to you on the back of a stamp, what would you write?

Note: there is a Greek word which means 'a short statement of faith' (or 'message'). It is *kerygma*.

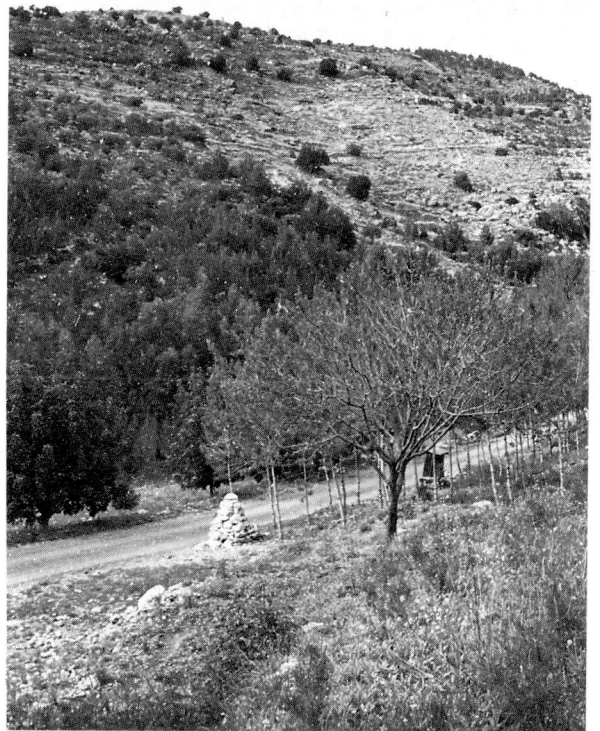

A road leading from Jerusalem

23·PENTECOST

The word 'Pentecost' comes from a Greek word meaning fiftieth. The festival or celebration called Pentecost occurs fifty days after the Jewish Passover and the Christian Easter. It has various other names.

Jewish

To Jews, Pentecost is also known as the Feast of Weeks or Shavuot. It is an early harvest festival which celebrates the wheat harvest. Two loaves of bread, made from newly-harvested wheat, were taken to the Temple as a sign of gratitude for the harvest. Nowadays, it is more important to Jews as a time for remembering how God gave them the Ten Commandments (see page 33) when they were in the wilderness. The Ten Commandments and the story of how they were received by Moses on Mount Sinai is read in synagogues at this time of year.

Christian

For Christians, Pentecost is the birthday of their church, and they remember what happened to the eleven apostles at the first Pentecost after the resurrection.

In Britain, it is sometimes called Whitsun (or White Sunday). This is because it used to be a popular day on which to hold baptism services and the people who were being baptised would wear white.

ACTS OF THE APOSTLES

After the four Gospels, the next book in the New Testament is The Acts of the Apostles. It tells of the 'acts' (or deeds) of the apostles in the years after the life of Jesus on earth. It was written by Luke, perhaps forty or fifty years after the events it describes.

In chapter 2 of Acts, read Luke's account of the first Pentecost after the resurrection of Jesus.

Christians believe that at that moment a special power came into the apostles; the power of the Holy Spirit. Christians say the Holy Spirit (sometimes called Holy Ghost) comes from God and is *part* of God; and gives strength to believers.

Whatever did happen in that room that day, it gave the apostles courage. They went out into Jerusalem, and there Simon Peter spoke to the crowds.

Because it was an important festival, many Jews had come to Jerusalem, including those who did not speak the language spoken by the apostles – yet when Peter spoke (according to Luke), everyone 'heard them speak in his own language'.

Luke goes on to say that, because of what Peter said, 3000 people believed that Jesus came from God, was crucified and then came back to life. You can read the whole story in chapter 2 of The Acts of the Apostles.

Projects

1 Suppose you were a foreigner in Jerusalem that day of Pentecost. Write a story about what you saw and heard.
2 If there had been a Radio Jerusalem in those days, how might it have reported the events of that Pentecost?

ROMAN CATHOLICS

Roman Catholic Christians believe their history goes back to Simon whom Jesus called Peter (or 'the Rock'). 'On this rock I will build my church,' said Jesus.

After Pentecost Peter went on several journeys, preaching. It is said that he settled in Rome and became leader (or *bishop*) of the church there. Another name for the Bishop of Rome or leader of the Roman Catholic Church is 'Pope'. Catholics say that whoever is Pope is the direct successor of Peter. The word 'catholic' means 'universal'. The Roman Catholic Church is a world-wide church with its headquarters in the Vatican in Rome.

PENTECOSTAL CHRISTIANS

This group of Christians is one of the fastest-growing churches. Pentecostalists believe that, like the apostles at Pentecost, they have received the gift of the Holy Spirit and that some have the gift of 'speaking in tongues'. Sometimes this speech can be recognised as a foreign language; other times it is a series of strange cries and sounds. Some Pentecostalists have the gift of 'interpreting' these sounds. Pentecostal churches sometimes have names like 'Assembly of God' or 'Elim Church'.

The local church

Christians use the word 'church' to mean:
   i) a church building and
   ii) a group of Christians.

How many different churches (buildings, including chapels, cathedrals, etc.) are there in your area? Mark them on a map, perhaps with different coloured flags or pins. Do you know of any 'churches' which are groups of Christians who do not meet in a church building but in an ordinary home?

Conclusions

Why is Pentecost an important festival for Jews?
Why is Pentecost an important festival for Christians?

Pope Paul VI (left) in Rome

55

24·THE CONVERSION OF PAUL

This is the first of a group of four units in which we shall be finding out about the life and teaching of one of the most important Christians who ever lived: Paul of Tarsus.

YOUNG SAUL

Yes, Saul – because Saul is the Hebrew or Jewish version of the Greek name Paul. But why was this man known as both Saul and Paul?

Saul (or Paul) was a Jew but somehow his family had also been given the very great honour of Roman citizenship. This meant that they had all sorts of privileges wherever they went throughout the Roman Empire. Saul grew up in a large city called Tarsus, in what is now Turkey. It was an important city: a trading centre with a university. And Tarsus was a place where Greeks lived and taught. So Saul was a Jew and a Roman – who spoke Greek (and other languages) and was known by Greek-speakers as Paul.

But what else do we know about him?

'The young Saul was sent to school in Jerusalem, where he studied under the famous Rabbi Gamaliel. He joined the party of the Pharisees, and was eager to keep the Jewish law in all its details. He was probably in Jerusalem at the time of Jesus' ministry and death, but there is no record of him having met Jesus then.'

Saul was perhaps five, perhaps fifteen, years younger than Jesus would have been, if Jesus had been still on earth. Some time after that Pentecost when Peter had first preached openly about Jesus, Saul noticed that many Jews were becoming followers of Jesus. One of them was a man called Stephen.

'When Saul heard Stephen preaching, he was certain of one thing: he hated the followers of Jesus. They were encouraging people to break God's law, he thought. And how could a man who had been crucified like a criminal be God's messiah? The Christians, he decided, must be

An impression of Paul in later life, drawn by Brian Robins

stamped out before they gained any more influence.'

Stephen, who had become a leading Christian, spoke enthusiastically to the Sanhedrin (see page 43) about Jesus. You can find out just what happened as a result of this speech if you read Acts of the Apostles 7:54 to 8:3.

Points to note:

1 Was the stoning an official, planned punishment?

2 What part did Saul play in it?

3 What two things happened to the Christians in Jerusalem as a result of all this?

56

To talk about...

What do you think of young Saul? Likeable? Fair? Holy? What is good about him?

On the Damascus road

Read Acts 9:1–2.

In groups, discuss

(a) what sort of mood Saul was in, and

(b) why do you think he needed letters to take with him from the high priest to the leaders of the synagogues in Damascus? What do you think those letters said?

In your group, write a short letter that the high priest (who was, remember, part of the Sanhedrin) might have given to Saul to carry with him to Damascus.

Conversion

The word 'conversion' means 'change'. A very great change came over Saul on his way to Damascus.

In his book, The Acts of the Apostles, Luke describes it in chapter 9:3–9; and also includes Saul's (or Paul's) memory of the event (22:3–11).

Read these two accounts. Working with a partner, make a list of the points they have in common.

Now read on in the first account in Acts (up to 9:16).

Improvisation

Work in threes. One of you is Ananias, one another Christian who lives in Damascus and knows nothing about Saul; and the third is a Christian who has just escaped from Jerusalem.

Begin your improvised scene with Ananias telling the other two about his dream. What advice do the other two then give Ananias?

Now read on again (9:17–22).

Work in groups of four or five. One is Saul, one is Ananias; the others are Christians in Damascus. Saul wants to find out all he can about Jesus and what the Christians believe; the others may or may not trust him yet, and want to find out all they can about him.

Improvise the scene. Later, one group might show their version to the others. What have they included that probably did happen? Have they missed anything out?

To talk about...

How does Saul seem to have altered? What is different about him? Does he say anything about his blindness?

How do you explain the change (or conversion) that came about in Saul? What does Saul now *believe*?

25·PAUL'S JOURNEYS

Following his conversion to Christianity and his escape from Damascus, Saul went to Jerusalem. Not surprisingly, the Christians there were at first suspicious of him. Was it a trick? Was the man who had allowed Stephen to be killed and who had imprisoned many Christians really now a Christian himself?

Eventually a Christian called Barnabas persuaded them that Saul was genuine. Soon after this, Saul returned to his home town, Tarsus. So far as we know, he spent the next ten years there, probably preaching and also working at his trade: he was a tent-maker.

From now on, he was known by the Greek (or Roman) version of his name, Paul.

One early description of Paul has survived (which may or may not be accurate): 'A short man, with a bald head and crooked legs; his body is fit and healthy; his eyebrows meet over his nose, which is rather hooked; his face is full of friendliness...'

Whatever he looked like, he was an enthusiastic believer and preacher.

Paul was an energetic man. Once he believed in Jesus, he set out to persuade others that Jesus was the Messiah, the Saviour the Jews had been waiting for. But he did not preach only to Jews: Paul took the faith to anyone who would listen.

He undertook three major preaching journeys; first in what is now southern Turkey and Cyprus; secondly, he toured right round 'Turkey' or Asia Minor and then into Greece; and then made a third journey to many of the same places, making new converts and renewing contacts with people he had met earlier.

And he also kept in touch with these people by writing to them. For example, while visiting Corinth in Greece he wrote to the Christians in Thessalonika; and then when he was in Ephesus he wrote to the Christians at Corinth.

The three journeys

Journey	Year (CE)	Reference
First	46–47	Acts 13 and 14
Second	50–52	Acts 15:36–18:22
Third	52–56	Acts 18:23–21:15

Copy out the table, and add two extra columns: 'Travelling companions' and 'Places visited'. Use the information on these pages to fill in these two columns.

By the time Paul returned from his first journey, so many Gentiles had become Christian that Jewish Christians began to be worried. They said that people who became Christians should also keep all the Jewish laws. A meeting was held in Jerusalem to discuss the matter and eventually it was agreed that Christians did not have to follow all Jewish laws and customs. However, many Jewish Christians continued to go to the synagogue on the Sabbath (Saturday) as well as meeting with Christians on Sunday to celebrate the day they believed Jesus rose from the dead. Paul often visited (and preached in) a synagogue when visiting a new town.

The third journey

Trace or make your own map of the eastern Mediterranean Sea (from the map shown here). Mark on it the route of Paul's third journey which was as follows:

From Antioch (in Syria)
by land to Ephesus;
by sea to Troas;
by sea to Philippi;
by land to Thessalonika;
by sea to Corinth;
by land to Beroea;
by land to Philippi;
by sea to Troas;
by sea to Miletus;
by sea to Patara;
by sea to Tyre.

Working with a partner and using the scale shown on the map, estimate the length in kilometres of each journey (approximately).

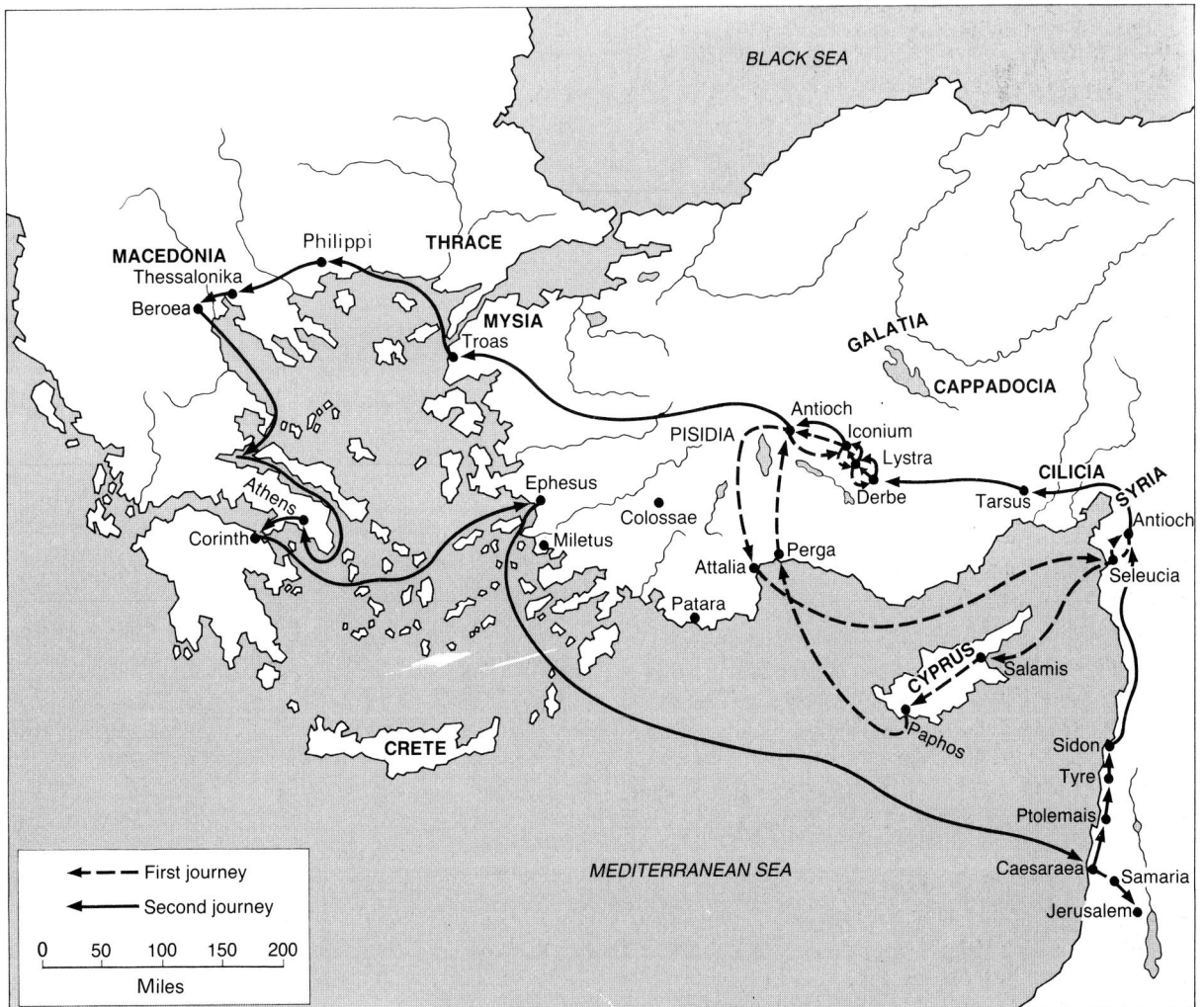

Paul's missionary journeys

26·PAUL'S LETTERS

We have seen that Paul was a great traveller. We have also seen that he kept in touch with the people he had met and who had become Christian, by sending them letters. Paul's letters are sometimes known by an old word for letter: Epistle. He probably wrote (or rather, dictated) many epistles or letters. Thirteen survive and are included in the New Testament. Eight were written while he was on his second and third journeys. For instance, while he was staying in Ephesus, he wrote to the Christians in Corinth, whom he had visited earlier.

Corinth

In this scene, two foreign sailors visit Corinth. The first one has never visited the port before. (You could all rehearse this scene in groups of four, and then one or more groups could present their version to the others.)

Sailor 1: So this is Corinth! We'll be all right here.

Sailor 2: You never put in here before then?

Sailor 1: No, worse luck. The ships I've worked on 've always sailed east – to Rhodes, Cyprus, round that way. First time I've come west. But I've heard plenty about Corinth.

Sailor 2: So you've heard about the prices then?

Sailor 1: What do you mean, the prices?

Sailor 2: What they charge. For anything. Everything.

Sailor 1: Uh?

Sailor 2: I'll show you (*calling*) Oi, you!

Greek: You're calling me, sailor?

Sailor 2: Yeah. Can you tell us where we can get a flask of wine?

Greek: It'll cost you.

Sailor 1: Course it'll cost us. We don't mind paying for a cup of wine.

Greek: No, I mean the information will cost you . . .

Sailor 2: See what I mean? You know, the Romans have a saying, on account of Corinth being a bit pricey, Corinth, they say, Corinth doesn't fit into everyone's pocket.

Drunk (*approaching*): Hic . . . would . . . either of you two fine . . . young hic . . . men, would either of you lend a poor old man a few coins for just a little . . . drink . . . hic?

Sailor 1: Ger-rout of it. Go on! What a place! What people! Here! My purse! Where's my purse? It was tied on to my belt. It's gone.

Sailor 2: That's something else I forgot to tell you. Thieves. There's a lot of thieves in Corinth. Corinthian cut-purses they call 'em.

It was among these people that Paul preached about Jesus when he visited Corinth on his second journey. What do you think *his* first visit to Corinth was like? Improvise the scene or describe it in a story.

Remember: during his stay there, many Corinthians became Christians.

PAUL'S FIRST LETTER TO THE CORINTHIANS

Some of Paul's letters are not all that easy to understand. One reason is that many are *answers* to news or letters that Paul has received from the various places. Reading them is a little bit like listening to one end of a telephone conversation: you have to guess what is being said at the other end.

This is how a modern Christian writer sees the letters:

66 They are mostly emergency writings, written off the cuff to answer special needs. Paul did not sit down to write them as one might sit down to write an article. He was clearly rampaging up and down the room 'giving out' at dictation speed. He can digress for a couple of paragraphs – or even a couple of chapters – before coming back to the matter in hand.

The end product is passionate, fiery and tempestuous, and does not make for easy reading. 99

Hubert Richards

These letters follow the same pattern of other letters written at that time. His first one to the Corinthians begins quite typically with an announcement of who it's from:

66 From Paul, who was called by the will of God to be an apostle of Christ, and from our colleague, Sosthenes– 99

We think Sosthenes may have been the leader of the synagogue in Corinth, who had become a Christian and was now living in Ephesus. Next comes the greeting.

66 To the Church of God which is in Corinth, to all who are called to be God's holy people, who belong to him in union with Christ Jesus, together with all people everywhere who worship our Lord Jesus Christ, their Lord and ours; may God our Father and the Lord Jesus Christ give you grace and peace. 99

Then comes a thanksgiving – and then Paul gets down to the main business of the letter.

And this includes one of the great messages of Paul's letters: that, as Jesus taught, we should love one another; we should care about each other.

One of its most famous passages is in chapter 13. Find it and read it. Why do you think that Paul thought it was necessary to send this letter to Corinth?

61

27·PAUL IN ROME

After Paul's third journey around the Mediterranean, he returned to Jerusalem. You will remember that his preaching (and that of other Christians) had already caused problems between Jews and Christians (see page 58). It was to do so again, including one day when Paul was teaching in the Temple in Jerusalem.

Man (*whisper*): Look over there – you know who that is?
Woman (*whisper*): It's Paul! The wicked old–
Man (*shouting*): Look everyone! Over there! (*Sensation*) It's Paul. That's the man that goes everywhere persuading Jews to forget about Moses and the prophets and to worship Jesus!
Woman: He's the man who brings the heathen into the temple! Seize him!
Man: Seize him!

In the book, The Acts of the Apostles, Luke tells us exactly what happened next:

66 The people all ran together, seized Paul and dragged him out of the temple. The mob was trying to kill him when a report was sent to the commander of the Roman troops that all Jerusalem was rioting. The commander took some officers and soldiers and rushed down to the crowd. 99

The Roman commander arrested Paul in order to protect him from the crowds.

A prisoner in Jerusalem

Paul was charged with causing a riot wherever he went, so he was kept in prison.

Eventually, after about two years, Paul asked to be tried in Rome, in front of the Emperor – and this was his right, as a Roman citizen. The local Roman governor was reluctant to allow this to happen: Paul after all was not a serious criminal, and the governor would seem pretty useless if he could not sort out the argument locally.

In the end, Paul got his way. About the year 60 CE, he was sent (under arrest) by ship to Rome. Luke travelled with him. It was an adventurous journey, including a shipwreck on the coast of the island of Malta. You can read about this voyage in The Acts of the Apostles 27 and 28. (If you have made your own map of his three missionary journeys, you could add the course of this voyage to it.)

A Roman slave badge

PAUL IN ROME

Once in Rome, Paul was technically a prisoner, waiting to defend himself in a trial to be held in front of the Roman Emperor. He was not in a prison, but was under house arrest. That is, he was allowed to rent his own house but he was kept in chains inside it, under the guard of a Roman soldier.

He was allowed visitors – such as other Jews who lived in Rome, who came to hear him preach. And he was also allowed to send letters.

Paul, Philemon and Onesimos

One of those letters was a very short one, not much more than a postcard, which Paul sent to a man called Philemon. Philemon was a wealthy and important citizen of Colossae and had become a Christian when Paul had preached there.

In those days, a rich man could buy slaves, in a slave market. They became his property and he could treat them as he wished. Some slave owners treated their slaves well; others did not. One of Philemon's slaves was called Onesimos (pronounced O – 'ness – i – muss). For some reason, Onesimos had run away to Rome (we do not know why). In Rome he had met Paul and become a Christian.

As Paul was under house arrest, Onesimos became very useful to him, going errands and so on. This leads to a terrible joke: the Greek name Onesimos means 'Useful'. So we can perhaps nickname him 'Andy . . .

Eventually, Paul decided he must send Onesimos back to his owner:

Onesimos: . . . So why can't I stay? You can't go out, I can.

Paul: But you belong with Philemon. You're still his slave.

Onesimos: He wouldn't mind if he knew where I was. He likes you. He'd want me to help you.

Paul: But that's the point. He doesn't know where you are. And I wouldn't keep you without permission.

Onesimos: If I go back, he could have me put to death. For running away in the first place.

Paul: Do you really think he would do that? He is a Christian.

Onesimos: Will you write a letter to him, that I can take with me?

Paul: Of course.

Onesimos: Telling him to let me off?

Paul: In my letter, I shall *ask* him to receive you back, not as a slave but as a brother, a fellow Christian.

Onesimos (*incredulous*): Equal with him? Me? A slave?

Paul: We are all equal in the sight of Jesus.

Onesimos: Even so, I'd like to stay here.

Paul: Your place is with Philemon. Yes, you must go, even if I'd like you to stay. Especially as you are . . .'Andy!

The postcard to Philemon

Suppose it really was a postcard that Paul sent to Philemon. Write that postcard for Paul.

What do you think Philemon said or did when Onesimos was sent back to him with Paul's epistle? (What is suggested by the fact that the letter has been preserved?) Perhaps you could improvise the scene or write Philemon's reply to Paul.

Conclusions

What did Paul believe about Jesus?
What were the 'foundations' of his faith?
Without Paul's travels, preaching and letters, what might have happened to Christianity?
In what ways can his teaching and writing be said to be part of the foundations of Christianity?
(Or, why is Paul important to Christians?)

Acknowledgements

The author and publishers wish to acknowledge the following photograph sources: Anglia TV p. 6; Ashmolean Museum, Oxford p. 51; Illustration of Paul by Brian Robins reproduced from 'Religion and Life' (Autumn 1974) with the permission of BBC Enterprises Ltd p. 56; BBC/Filmstrip Services Ltd p. 28; BBC Hulton Picture Library p. 50; Camera Press pp. 14, 47 (top and bottom), 60; Camerapix Hutchison p. 17 (R), 26; J. Allan Cash Ltd pp. 15, 32, 36 (R); Bruce Coleman Ltd p. 27; Barbara Edwards/Mary Evans Picture Library p. 5 (R); Mary Evans Picture Library pp. 22, 42; Sonia Halliday pp. 38 (L), 48 (T); Hutchison Picture Library p. 38 (R); Jewish Education Bureau p. 35 (B); Mansell Collection p. 62; Methodist Church Missionary Society p. 12; Netherlands National Tourist Office p. 20; Ann and Bury Peerless p. 30; Photo Library International, Cover; Photo Source pp. 4 (B), 7, 55; Popperfoto pp. 13, 31; Ronald Sheridan's Photo-Library p. 53; N. Thiagarajan p. 17 (L); Woodmansterne Ltd pp. 36 (L), 37 (T); Zefa Picture Library (UK) Ltd pp. 18, 33, 35 (T), 37 (B).

The author and publishers wish to acknowledge the following, whose copyright material has been used: the Board of Deputies of British Jews for quotations from Clive Lawton, *The Jewish People; some questions answered*; Eyre Methuen for an extract from Bertolt Brecht's play *The Life of Galileo*; trans. Desmond I. Vesey (1963); Hulton for a quotation from Rosalyn A. Kendrick, *Setting the Foundations* (1983); Oxford University Press for a quotation from Roderick Hunt, *Ghosts, Witches and Things Like That* (1984); RMEP for a quotation from Howard Marsh, *Divali* (1982).

The publishers have made every effort to trace the copyright holders, but where they have failed to do so they will be pleased to make the necessary arrangements at the first opportunity.

Artwork: Illustra Design

First published 1987
Reprinted 1988

Published by
MACMILLAN EDUCATION LTD
Houndmills, Basingstoke, Hampshire RG21 2XS
and London
Companies and representatives
throughout the world

Designed by Nina J. Nadolski-Birks

Printed in Hong Kong

British Library Cataloguing in Publication Data
Self, David
Foundations of faith. — (The Macmillan
religious education course; bk.1)
1. Religions
I. Title
291   BL80.2
ISBN 0-333-39216-7